A Continuous Harmony

Books by Wendell Berry

Wendell Berry / A Continuous Harmony

ESSAYS CULTURAL AND AGRICULTURAL

A Harvest/HBJ Book
Harcourt Brace Jovanovich, Publishers
San Diego   New York   London

The lines from "Corson's Inlet" are from *Corsons Inlet: A Book of Poems* by A. R. Ammons, copyright © 1965 by Cornell University, reprinted by permission of Cornell University Press; from "Directive," *The Poetry of Robert Frost*, edited by Edward Connery Lathem, copyright 1947, © 1969 by Holt, Rinehart and Winston, Inc., reprinted by permission of Holt, Rinehart and Winston, Inc.; from "The Novices," *O Taste and See* by Denise Levertov, copyright © 1964 by Denise Levertov Goodman, reprinted by permission of New Directions Publishing Corporation; from "Written on the Wall at Chang's Hermitage," *One Hundred Poems from the Chinese* by Kenneth Rexroth, all rights reserved, reprinted by permission of New Directions Publishing Corporation; from "Asphodel, that Greeny Flower," "Deep Religious Faith," and "The Host," *Pictures from Breughel and Other Poems* by William Carlos Williams, copyright © 1955 by William Carlos Williams, from "Paterson," *Paterson, Book I* by William Carlos Williams, copyright 1946 by William Carlos Williams, from "To Elsie," *Collected Earlier Poems* by William Carlos Williams, copyright 1938 by William Carlos Williams, reprinted by permission of New Directions Publishing Corporation; from "The Island," *Collected Poems* by Edwin Muir, copyright © 1960 by Willa Muir, reprinted by permission of Oxford University Press, Inc.; from "Piute Creek" by Gary Snyder, copyright © 1965 by Gary Snyder, reprinted by permission; from "Identity" by A. R. Ammons, *Southern Poetry Review: A Decade of Poems*, copyright © 1969 by Southern Poetry Review Press at North Carolina State University, reprinted by permission, and in *Expressions of Sea Level* by A. R. Ammons, Ohio State University Press; from "Shadows," *The Complete Poems of D. H. Lawrence*, edited by Vivian de Sola Pinto and F. Warren Roberts, copyright © 1964, 1971 by Angelo Ravagli and C. M. Weekley, Executors of the Estate of Frieda Lawrence Ravagli. All rights reserved. Reprinted by permission of The Viking Press, Inc.

Library of Congress Cataloging in Publication Data

Berry, Wendell, date
  A continuous harmony.

  (A Harvest book, HB 301)
  CONTENTS: A secular pilgrimage.— Notes from an absence and a return.
—A homage to Dr. Williams. [etc.]
  I. Title.
[PS3552.E75C6 1975] 814′.5′4 74-17016
ISBN 0-15-622575-1 (Harvest/HBJ : pbk.)

Printed in the United States of America
D E F G H I J

For Anne and Harry Caudill

Some of the essays in this volume previously appeared in *Apple, The Courier-Journal & Times Magazine, The Hudson Review, Kentucky English Bulletin, Lillabulero, The Southern Review, Whole Earth Catalog.*

Contents

From the beginning we had seen virtually no wilderness. Rice terraces had climbed thousands of feet up hillsides, prayer flags flapped at the passes; paths occasionally edged with mani walls crisscrossed the country. For all the size, for all the intransigent power of the ice-crusted wall to the north, wilderness, as western man defines it, did not exist. Yet there was no impression of nature tamed. It seemed to me that here man lived in continuous harmony with the land, as much and as briefly a part of it as all its other occupants. He used the earth with gratitude, knowing that care was required for continued sustenance. He rotated crops, controlled the cutting of wood, bulwarked his fields against erosion. In this peaceful co-existence, man was the invited guest.

—THOMAS F. HORNBEIN,
Everest: The West Ridge

I wish to thank my colleagues of the College of Arts and Sciences of the University of Kentucky for free time which permitted me to write the long essay "Discipline and Hope." A portion of that essay was offered at the University of Kentucky as the Distinguished Professor Lecture on November 17, 1971.

A Continuous Harmony

A Secular Pilgrimage

One of the most exciting and vital kinds of poetry being written now in this country is nature poetry. There is some danger of oversimplification in saying so, for you will not find many poets, if any, who are writing only about nature; those who are writing the best nature poems are also writing well on other subjects: the city, love, marriage, politics, war, history, art, and so on. But running through the work of such poets as Gary Snyder, Denise Levertov, and A. R. Ammons,* there is a sustained attentiveness to nature and to the relation between man and nature.

---

* These poets are representative of the sort of interest in nature that I am talking about. I don't mean to imply either that they are our only nature poets or that they are the only ones whose work I value.

3

"Nature poetry" is a clumsy term, and it presents immediate difficulties, for there is a sense in which most poetry is nature poetry; most poets, even those least interested in nature, have found in the natural world an abundant stock of symbols and metaphors. But I will use the term here to refer only to those poets who seem to me to have turned to the natural world, not as a source of imagery, but as subject and inspiration—as Marvell and Wordsworth and Thoreau (in his prose) turned to it. With those men nature was of primary interest; by seeing into its life they sensed the presence of a shaping and sustaining spirit within it. With poets such as Donne or Pope or Shelley the particulars of nature were only of secondary interest insofar as they "stood for" an abstraction that interested the poet primarily and that he had in mind before he turned to nature for an image.

The nature poets of our own time characteristically approach their subject with an openness of spirit and imagination, allowing the meaning and the movement of the poem to suggest themselves out of the facts. Their art has an implicit and essential humility, a reluctance to impose on things as they are, a willingness to relate to the world as student and servant, a wish to be included in the natural order rather than to "conquer nature," a wish to discover the natural form rather than to create new forms that would be exclusively human. To create is to involve oneself as fully, as consciously and imaginatively, as possible in the creation, to be immersed in the world. In "Some Notes on Organic Form" Denise Levertov has said: "For me, back of the idea of organic form is the concept that there is a form in all things (and in our experience) which the poet can discover and reveal." "Form," she says, "is never more than the *revelation* of content." And she speaks of "a religious devotion to the truth, to the splendor of the authentic. . . ."

As I have already made clear, this poetry arises out of a state of mind that could very accurately be described as religious. I am probably giving that adjective a broader application than it usually has. My use of it might, I suppose, be defined as primitive. I would apply it, for instance, to the sense of the presence of mystery or divinity in the world, or even to the attitudes of wonder or awe or humility before the works of the creation. And I will not use the word here to refer to any of those revealed certainties that are so large a part of the lore of the various churches. A better term than religious might be worshipful, in the sense of *valuing* what one does not entirely understand, or aspiring beyond what may be known. There is a passage in John Stewart Collis's book *The Triumph of the Tree* that will serve perfectly as a definition of the state of mind I am talking about; he is speaking of primitive man:

Having become aware of objects and begun to name them, this Earliest Man became aware of something else. It is a remarkable fact that no sooner had he looked closely at the phenomena of Nature than he began to concern himself with, not the visible object in front of him which he could clearly see, but with an invisible object which he could not see at all. He looked at the trees, the rocks, the rivers, the animals, and having looked at them he at once began to talk about something *in them* which he had never seen and never heard of. This thing inside the objective appearance was called a god. No one forced man at this time to think about gods, there was no tradition imposing it upon him—and yet his first thoughts seem to have turned towards a Thing behind the thing, a Force behind or within the appearance. Thus *worship* . . .

The peculiar aspiration of the contemporary nature poetry might be fairly accurately suggested by calling it a secular pilgrimage—at least that is a phrase that has begun to accompany it in my own thinking. It is secular because it takes place outside of, or without reference to, the institutions of religion, and it does not seek any institutional shrine or holy place; it is in search of the world. But it is a pilgrimage nevertheless because it is a religious quest. It does not seek the world of inert materiality that is postulated both by the heaven-oriented churches and by the exploitive industries; it seeks the world of the creation, the created world in which the Creator, the formative and quickening spirit, is still immanent and at work. This sense of immanence is given memorably in two lines of Guy Davenport's long poem, *Flowers and Leaves*: ". . . the ghost who wears our inert rock/ is fanatic with metamorphosis. . . ."

I begin, then, with the assumption that perhaps the great disaster of human history is one that happened to or within religion: that is, the conceptual division between the holy and the world, the excerpting of the Creator from the creation. Collis is worth quoting again in this connection; though perhaps it may be argued that he is wrong about the cause, I think he is correct in his description of what happened:

. . . whereas under polytheism the gods were intimately connected with the earth, and stimulated veneration for it, under monotheism deity was extracted from the earth. God was promoted to higher regions. He went completely out of sight. It became possible to fear God without fearing Nature—nay, to love God (whatever was meant) and to hate his creations.

If God was not in the world, then obviously the world was a thing of inferior importance, or of no importance at all. Those who were disposed to exploit it were thus free to do so. And this split in public attitudes was inevitably mirrored in the lives of individuals: a man could aspire to heaven with his mind and his heart while destroying the earth, and his fellow men, with his hands.

The human or earthly problem has always been one of behavior, or morality: How should a man live in this world? Institutional Christianity has usually tended to give a non-answer to this question: He should live for the next world. Which completely ignores the *fact* that the here is antecedent to the hereafter, and that, indeed, the Gospels would seem to make one's fate in the hereafter dependent on one's behavior here. Some varieties of Christianity have held that one should despise the things of this world—which made it all but mandatory that they should be neglected as well. In that way men of conscience—or men who might reasonably have been expected to be men of conscience—have been led to abandon the world, and their own posterity, to the exploiters and ruiners. So exclusively focused on the hereafter, they have been neither here nor there.

This schism in man's sense of himself was protested at the end of the eighteenth century by William Blake, who wrote (of the time when "the whole creation will be consumed and appear infinite and holy"): "But first the notion that man has a body distinct from his soul is to be expunged. . . ." It was protested by Henry David Thoreau, who wrote in his journal on June 21, 1840: "The body is the first proselyte the Soul makes. Our life is but the Soul made known by its fruits, the body. The whole duty of man may be expressed in one line—Make to yourself a perfect body." And it has been protested in our own time by the Welsh clergyman R. S. Thomas, in his poem, "The Minister":

Is there no passion in Wales? There is none
Except in the racked hearts of men like Morgan,
Condemned to wither and starve in the cramped cell
Of thought their fathers made them.
Protestantism—the adroit castrator
Of art; the bitter negation
Of song and dance and the heart's innocent joy—
You have botched our flesh and left us only the soul's
Terrible impotence in a warm world.

The contempt for the world or the hatred of it, which is exemplified both by the wish to exploit it for the sake of cash and by the willingness to despise it for the sake of "salvation," has reached a terrifying climax in our own time. The rift between soul and body, the Creator and the creation, has admitted the entrance into the world of the machinery of the world's doom. We no longer feel ourselves threatened by the God-made doomsday of Revelation, or by the natural world's-end foreseen by science. We face an apocalypse of *our own* making—a man-made cosmic terror. The old-fashioned doomsdays of religion and nature were terrifying enough for mere humans, perhaps, but looking back from the perspective of our own time, we can see that their meanings were not entirely negative. The doomsday of God, as described in the Bible, in spite of the terror and the destruction, was at the same time to be the triumph of divinity, of virtue, of spiritual value. In the doomsday of nature, the burning out of the sun or whatever, the life of the world would presumably be survived by natural law, the cosmic forces that brought it into being in the first place, and might bring into being another of the same kind or a better. But the doomsday of man is creation in reverse. Should we accomplish the destruction we are now capable of, we will destroy not only ourselves and the world, but also whatever right we may once have had to live. Doubtless many men have come, like Job, to wish that they had never been born. But until ours, no generation ever had to face the possibility that its extinction at birth might have been a benefit to the world. Such is the drastic and fearful change we have made in our life and in our sense of ourselves. How did it happen? It could only have happened by our failure to care enough for the world, to be humble enough before it, to think competently enough of its welfare. Rather than be ruled by the thought of the world's good, which is identical with our own most meaningful good, we have set up the false standards of national interest, power, production, personal comfort or pride or greed—or the desire to get to heaven, which, if it involves neglect of the life of the world, becomes only a rarefied form of gluttony.

Do we really hate the world? Are we really contemptuous of it? Have we really ignored its nature and its needs and the problems of its health? The evidence against us is everywhere. It is in our wanton and thoughtless misuse of the land and the other natural resources, in our wholesale pollution of the water and air, in strip mining, in our massive use and misuse of residual poisons in agriculture and elsewhere, in our willingness to destroy whole landscapes in the course of what we call "construction" and "progress," in the earth-destroying and population-destroying weapons we use in our wars, in the planet-destroying weapons now ready for use in the arsenals of the most powerful and violent nations of the world. It is in our hatred of races and nations. It is in our willingness to honor profit above everything except victory. It is in our willingness to spend more on war than on everything else. It is in our unappeasable restlessness, our nomadism, our anxiousness to get to another place or to "the top" or "somewhere" or to heaven or to the moon.

Our hatred of the world is most insidiously and dangerously present in the constantly widening discrepancy between our power and our needs, our means and our ends. This is because of machinery and what we call efficiency. In order to build a road we destroy several thousand acres of farmland forever, all in perfect optimism, without regret, believing that we have gained much and lost nothing. In order to build a dam, which like all human things will be temporary, we destroy a virgin stream forever, believing that we have conquered nature and added significantly to our stature. In order to burn cheap coal we destroy a mountain forever, believing, in the way of lovers of progress, that what is of immediate advantage to us must be a permanent benefit to the universe. Fighting in Vietnam in the interest, as we say and would have ourselves believe, of the Vietnamese people, we have destroyed their villages, their croplands, their forests, herded the people into concentration camps, and in every way diminished the possibility of life in that country; and the civilian casualties are vastly greater than the military. In order to protect ourselves against Russia or China, or whoever our enemy will be in ten years, we have prepared weapons the use of which will, we know, involve our own destruction and the destruction of the world as well. Great power has always been blinding to those who wield it. Those who follow blindly in the wake of their own power practice hypocrisy by reflex; it is their natural camouflage. And in this age of super machines and super weapons hypocrisy is not only sinful, it is probably suicidal.

A man cannot hate the world and hate his own kind without hating himself. The familiar idea that a man's governing religious obligation is to "save" himself, procure *for himself* an eternal life, is based on a concept of individualism that is both vicious and absurd. And this religious concept is the counterpart, and to a considerable extent the cause, of the vicious secular individualism that suggests that a man's governing obligation is to enrich himself in this world. But man cannot live alone— he cannot have values alone, religious or otherwise, any more than he can live by bread alone. Such desires can live only at the world's expense and at the expense of one's own earthly life, which one inevitably devalues in devaluing the earth. So when a man seeks to live on the earth only for the eternal perpetuation, or only for the economic enrichment, of a life that he has devalued and despised, he is involved not only in absurdity but in perversion—a perversion that has now become the deadly disease of the world.

In *The Triumph of the Tree*, Collis outlines a most useful and clarifying historical scheme. First, he says, there was the "Era of Mythology," when men believed that they should venerate the world because it was inhabited by spirits and gods; they were frugal and considerate in their use of the world for fear of offending the resident divinities. Next came the "Era of Economics" when the creation began to be valued in terms of cash; the sacred groves were cut down and, since the gods took no direct revenge, the trees were sawed into lumber and put up for sale. This era built into an orgy of exploitation that has now "brought us to the edge of disaster."At this point we may, *if* we are able to make ourselves wise enough and humble enough, enter an "Era of Ecology," when we will utilize "the science of achieving an equilibrium with the environment." We will be as protective of the natural world as our primitive forebears, but this time for reasons that are knowledgeable and conscious rather than superstitious. We will realize and live in the realization that nature is not inexhaustible and that, in fact, we have already used up more than our share of its wealth. We will realize that we do not live *on* the earth, but with and within its life. We will realize that the earth is not dead, like the concept of property, but as vividly and intricately alive as a man or a woman, and that there is a delicate interdependence between its life and our own. We will take for granted what our farmers have had to learn with surprise and pain and to their cost, and what most politicians and businessmen have never learned: it is not the area of a country that makes its value or its most meaningful strength, but its life, the depth and richness of its topsoil.

But Collis's vision of this last era, this future in which man may live in harmony with the world, is not merely scientific, though science will provide many of the necessary insights and methods; his vision is also religious. He accepts the contemporary decline of the organized religions, and finds hope in it:

Both polytheism and monotheism have done their work. The images are broken, the idols are all overthrown. This is now regarded as a very irreligious age. But perhaps it only means that the mind is moving from one state to another. The next stage is not a belief in many gods. It is not a belief in one god. It is not a belief at all—not a conception in the intellect. It is an extension of consciousness so that we may *feel* God, or, if you will, an experience of harmony, an intimation of the Divine, which will link us again with *animism*, the experience of unity lost at the in-break of self-consciousness. This will atone for our sin (which means *separation*); it will be our at-one-ment.

And here I can go back to the subject of poetry, for it is clear that if such an era is to be achieved—and it is either that or the apocalypse of technology—it will not be by the mechanical obedience of most men to new rules set up by a few. In the first place, men do not often obey mechanically; they tend to be good only insofar as they understand goodness. Much of our present destructiveness, for instance, is in defiance of rules that have been in existence for many years, but whose applicability to present lives has been blurred by new circumstances or obscured by old rhetoric. If the rules are to apply and be observed, they must not only be written and publicized and learned, but understood, *felt*, accommodated to the particularities of the lives of particular people. If it is well to consider the needs of the earth as one's own needs, that must be carried beyond abstraction into the specific relation between each man and his place in the world. There must be new contact between men and the earth; the earth must be newly seen and heard and felt and smelled and tasted; there must be a renewal of the wisdom that comes with knowing clearly the pain and the pleasure and the risk and the responsibility of being alive in this world. This is only to say that such an era, like all eras, will arrive and remain by the means of a new speech—a speech that will cause the world to live and thrive in men's minds.

"Poetry," Thoreau said, "is nothing but healthy speech. . . ." By which he meant, I suppose, speech that is not only healthy in itself, but conducive to the health of the speaker, giving him a true and vigorous relation to the world.

In the first of his books on haiku, R. H. Blyth says: "Poetry is that excess, that over-abundance which makes morality bearable and virtue alive. . . ." Also: "Poetry is a return to nature: to our own nature, to that of each thing, and to that of all things." Also: "Poetry is interpenetration"—and he quotes Marcus Aurelius, a passage that could have been written by an ecologist in our own day: "All things are interwoven each with [the] other: the tie is sacred, and nothing, or next to nothing is alien to aught else." And poetry, Blyth says, is that sacred tie. To complete his thought, he is emphatic in refusing to account for poetry in purely literary terms: "Poetry is not the words written in a book, but the mode of activity of the mind of the poet." In other words, it is not only a technique and a medium, but a power as well, a power to apprehend the unity, the sacred tie, that holds life together.

The poetry of this century, like the world in this century, has suffered from the schism in the modern consciousness. It has been turned back upon itself, fragmented, obscured in its sense of its function. Like all other human pursuits, it has had to suffer, and to some extent enact, the modern crisis: the failure of the past to teach us to deal with the present or to envision and prepare for a desirable future. It has often seemed to lack wholeness and wisdom. One is tempted to say that some poets have grown too civilized, have become hive poets. In his book *Spring in Washington*, Louis J. Halle expresses some strong reservations about the hive mentality:

It is curious how the preoccupations of the hive fill us, driving out all memory of the universe into which we were born. Perhaps the whole human race may be said to suffer from amnesia, not knowing whence it came or why it finds itself here. But we inhabitants of the hive suffer from double amnesia, one case within another, and are removed one stage further from the ultimate reality in which we have our beginning and our end. We have forgotten that we live in the universe, and that our civilization itself is merely an elaboration of the palm-leaf hat that one of our ancestors tried on ten thousand years ago to ward off the sun, a more complicated and ample version that now not only wards off the sun but shuts out the view. We have lost ourselves within it.

Thomas Merton wrote that the "new consciousness which isolates man in his own knowing mind and separates him from the world around him (which he does not know as it is in itself but only as it is in his mind) makes wisdom impossible because it severs the communion between subject and object, man and nature, upon which wisdom depends." But he says in the same essay that in Greek tragedy, the "catharsis of pity and terror delivers the participant from *hubris* and restores him to an awareness of his place in the scheme of things. . . ." I think that this is to a considerable degree true also of the best nature poetry, which seeks expressly the power to deepen our insight into the very relationship Merton is talking about. It seeks to give us a sense of our proper place in the scheme of things. Its impulse is toward the realization of the presence of other life. Man, it keeps reminding us, is the center of the universe only in the sense that wherever he is it *seems* to him that he is at the center of his own horizon; the truth is that he is only a part of a vast complex of life, on the totality and the order of which he is blindly dependent. Since that totality and order have never yet come within the rational competence of our race, and even now do not seem likely ever to do so, the natural effect of such poetry is the religious one of humility and awe. It does not seem farfetched to assume that this religious effect might, in turn, produce the moral effect of care and competence and frugality in the use of the world.

As I have already suggested, I think that there is a considerable body of contemporary nature poetry in existence in this country that incorporates the essential double awareness of the physical presence of the natural world and of the immanence of mystery or divinity in the physical presence. This poetry, of course, did not materialize solely out of the awareness of nature. It has an extensive poetical ancestry of which it is conscious, and I think one may go far toward saying what this new poetry is like by hypothesizing at some length about its ancestry. It will necessarily be hypothesizing, because the ancestors I will speak of are the ones that I happen to be most aware of myself; I think that they are likely ones, but I cannot guarantee that they are the ones best known to other poets.

Though English poetry is full of nature *imagery*, and though it has had a constant interest in one or another of the *concepts* of nature, it seems to me surprisingly seldom that the immediate and particular manifestations of nature are acknowledged and looked at for their own sake. The natural world does impinge powerfully and unforgettably upon the consciousness of Geoffrey Chaucer at the beginning of his Prologue to the *Canterbury Tales*; though he is setting off on a pilgrimage, he cannot resist the attraction of the flowers, the birdsong, the damp earth and fresh sunlight of the April morning. But so far as I know, nature was not so openly turned to again until, in the seventeenth century, Andrew Marvell wrote such poems as "The Garden" and "Upon Appleton House." In the latter, his most ambitious poem, there is a clear gradation or ascent from the purely human context of the house and its family heritage, to the domesticated nature of the fields along the river, to the forest. The poem is notable, for one reason among many others, because it shows clearly that Marvell was thoughtful of wild nature and valued it in a way that was rare in English poetry before the romantic period. As the poem moves from house to forest, his imagination quickens and he becomes more and more exuberant in both mood and imagery. In the stanza where he turns from the house to the fields, he makes a stunning acknowledgment of the wildness and mystery in nature; at this point the wildness is not so much in the scene but in an awesome power to change and transform that Marvell senses *in* the scene, suddenly, and apparently to his surprise, and which his imagination seizes upon and emulates:

And now to the Abbyss I pass
Of that unfathomable Grass,
Where Men like Grashoppers appear,
But Grashoppers are Gyants there . . .

And then, the fields having been mowed and grazed, the river floods, and Marvell takes "Sanctuary in the Wood," which he calls "this yet green, yet growing Ark." The wood he describes as a natural temple where one may read "*Natures mystick Book.*" And the poet emerges as a priest in another striking passage that is almost Whitmanian:

The Oak-Leaves me embroyder all,
Between which Caterpillars crawl:
And Ivy, with familiar trails,
Me licks, and clasps, and curles, and hales.
Under this *antick Cope* I move
Like some great *Prelate of the Grove* . . .

And there is at last complete submergence into this wild place; he becomes one with it, in a kind of baptism or planting or crucifixion:

Bind me ye *Woodbines* in your 'twines,
Curle me about ye gadding *Vines*,
And Oh so close your Circles lace,
That I may never leave this Place:
But, lest your Fetters prove too weak,
Ere I your Silken Bondage break,
Do you, *O Brambles*, chain me too,
And courteous *Briars* nail me through.

In the same century Henry Vaughan wrote poems that acknowledge, like the thirty-third Psalm, that "the earth is full of the goodness of the Lord." He apparently took to heart the exultant spirit of Psalm 104 where it is said that the Lord created the world "in wisdom" and that he rejoices in his work. It is as though he read literally Christ's admonition to "consider the lilies of the field, how they grow. . . ." In his poem "The Bird" he says, "All things that be praise Him, and had / Their lesson taught them when first made / . . . So hills and valleys into singing break. . . ." The very stones "are deep in admiration." And Thomas Traherne wrote in one of his prose meditations:

Suppose a river, or a drop of water, an apple or a sand, an ear of corn, or an herb: God knoweth infinite excellencies in it more than we: he seeth how it relateth to angels and men; how it proceedeth from the most perfect Lover to the most perfectly beloved; how it representeth all his attributes; how it conduceth in its place, by the best of means to the best of ends: and for this cause it cannot be beloved too much. God the Author and God the End is to be beloved in it; angels and men are to be beloved in it; and it is highly to be esteemed for all their sakes.

Later there came William Blake's well-known formula:

To see a World in a Grain of Sand
And a Heaven in a Wild Flower,
Hold Infinity in the palm of your hand
And Eternity in an hour.

William Wordsworth virtually made this his life's work—this reaching into the life of nature toward its informing spirit—

                                a dark
Inscrutable workmanship that reconciles
Discordant elements, makes them cling together
In one society.

This led him, in *The Prelude*, to an affirmation that is epic in both scale and statement:

Should the whole frame of earth by inward throes
Be wrenched, or fire come down from far to scorch
Her pleasant habitations, and dry up
Old Ocean, in his bed left singed and bare,

Yet would the Living Presence still subsist
Victorious, and composure would ensue,
And kindlings like the morning . . .

But though Wordsworth was preoccupied with the experience of nature, there is remarkably little in the way of particular observation to be found in him. What absorbed him was that Presence that loomed behind created things and was manifested in them. He was apparently able to "see into the life of things" without having to scrutinize very closely the things themselves.

Gerard Manley Hopkins, more conventionally religious than Wordsworth, had the same eagerness to thrust through appearances toward a realization of the divine. With Hopkins, this was not the anonymous Presence of Wordsworth's poems, but God, Jehovah, who broods over his creation in which his glory is manifest. But Hopkins was nevertheless a keener observer than Wordsworth; he loved the physical facts of nature, and took pains to capture their look and feel and movement. In the accuracy of his observation, and in the onomatopoeia of his diction and rhythms, he is clearly a forebear of the contemporary nature poets. "God's Grandeur" gives not only a sense of his technique but also of his critical values with respect to nature and civilization:

The world is charged with the grandeur of God.
It will flame out like shining from shook foil;
It gathers to a greatness like the ooze of oil
Crushed. Why do men then now not reck his rod?
Generations have trod, have trod, have trod;
And all is seared with trade; bleared, smeared with toil;

And wears man's smudge and shares man's smell: the soil
Is bare now, nor can foot feel, being shod.

The earliest American ancestor, among the poets, is
Walt Whitman. I think that some of our poets are very
close in attitude and affinity, though not often in manner, to these passages from "Song of Myself":

My tread scares the wood-drake and wood-duck, on my
     distant and day-long ramble;
They rise together—they slowly circle around.

I believe in those wing'd purposes,
And acknowledge red, yellow, white, playing within me,
And consider green and violet, and the tufted crown, in-
     tentional . . .
*
All truths wait in all things,
They neither hasten their own delivery nor resist it . . .
*
I believe a leaf of grass is no less than the journey work of
     the stars,
And that the pismire is equally perfect, and a grain of
     sand, and the egg of the wren . . .
*
I find I incorporate gneiss, coal, long-threaded moss,
     fruits, grains, esculent roots,
And am stucco'd with quadrupeds and birds all over . . .

Among the American poets who began writing early in
our own century, there was a prevalent distrust of abstractions, especially those abstractions that had begun

to be credited automatically by the society. They felt that men and the world had been poorly served by these abstractions, and it is clearer now than in their own time how right they were. But they also realized that men's minds were insulated and benumbed by their platitudes and clichés—blinded and deafened, exiled from the world. There is a memorable poem on this subject by Wallace Stevens; it is called "On the Road Home":

It was when I said,
"There is no such thing as the truth,"
That the grapes seemed fatter.
The fox ran out of his hole.

William Carlos Williams, in *Paterson*, said emphatically that man must turn to the world to learn whatever he would know:

—Say it, no ideas but in things—
nothing but the blank faces of the houses
and cylindrical trees
bent, forked by preconception and accident—
split, furrowed, creased, mottled, stained—
secret—into the body of the light!

In Canto LXXXI, Ezra Pound wrote some lines that could serve as the epigraph of the science of ecology. Again the message is to escape the abstractions; man will have to break out of the context of his own assumptions and measure himself by the truer measure of "the green world":

The ant's a centaur in his dragon world.
Pull down thy vanity, it is not man

Made courage, or made order, or made grace,
    Pull down thy vanity, I say pull down.
Learn of the green world what can be thy place . . .

And in a late poem entitled "Directive," Robert Frost
wrote both a proposal and an enactment of a secular pilgrimage—a return to the wilderness in order to be re-
stored, made whole, made one with nature. The poem is
explicitly religious, bearing allusions to the tenth chapter
of Matthew ("he that loseth his life . . . shall find it"),
to the eighteenth chapter of Matthew ("become as little
children"), to the healing water of Bethesda, to the communion and the Holy Grail. The poet appears frankly in
the role of priest, howbeit a slyly humorous one. Though
it is hardly a typical Frost poem, I think it is his best.

Back out of all this now too much for us,
Back in a time made simple by the loss
Of detail, burned, dissolved, and broken off
Like graveyard marble sculpture in the weather,
There is a house that is no more a house . . .

. . . .

Your destination and your destiny's
A brook that was the water of the house,
Cold as a spring as yet so near its source,
Too lofty and original to rage.
(We know the valley streams that when aroused
Will leave their tatters hung on barb and thorn.)
I have kept hidden in the instep arch
Of an old cedar at the waterside
A broken drinking goblet like the Grail

Under a spell so the wrong ones can't find it,
So can't get saved, as Saint Mark says they mustn't.
(I stole the goblet from the children's playhouse.)
Here are your waters and your watering place.
Drink and be whole again beyond confusion.

A more innately religious man than any of the four Americans I have just named, D. H. Lawrence was, I think, one of the best nature poets. He seems to have come very naturally to the role of priest-poet. I will quote his poem "Shadows," one of the *Last Poems,* written when he knew he was dying:

And if tonight my soul may find her peace
in sleep, and sink in good oblivion,
and in the morning wake like a new-opened flower
then I have been dipped again in God, and new-created.

And if, as weeks go round, in the dark of the moon
my spirit darkens and goes out, and soft strange gloom
pervades my movements and my thoughts and words
then I shall know that I am walking still
with God, we are close together now the moon's in
    shadow.

And if, as autumn deepens and darkens
I feel the pain of falling leaves, and stems that break in
    storms
and trouble and dissolution and distress
and then the softness of deep shadows folding, folding
round my soul and spirit, around my lips
so sweet, like a swoon, or more like the drowse of a low,
    sad song

singing darker than the nightingale, on, on to the solstice
and the silence of short days, the silence of the year, the
    shadow,
then I shall know that my life is moving still
with the dark earth, and drenched
with the deep oblivion of earth's lapse and renewal.

And if, in the changing phases of man's life
I fall in sickness and in misery
my wrists seem broken and my heart seems dead
and strength is gone, and my life
is only the leavings of a life:

and still, among it all, snatches of lovely oblivion, and
    snatches of renewal
odd, wintry flowers upon the withered stem, yet new,
    strange flowers
such as my life has not brought forth before, new
    blossoms of me—

then I must know that still
I am in the hands [of] the unknown God,
he is breaking me down to his own oblivion
to send me forth on a new morning, a new man.

Nearer to us was Theodore Roethke, who wrote, toward the end of his life, poems of visionary peacemaking
with the world. This is the ending of one called "Journey
to the Interior":

As a blind man, lifting a curtain, knows it is morning,
I know this change:

On one side of silence there is no smile;
But when I breathe with the birds,
The spirit of wrath becomes the spirit of blessing,
And the dead begin from their dark to sing in my sleep.

That gives a possible line of descent through the history of poetry in England and America. But before speaking of my contemporaries, I want to suggest two other influences that I think have come to be strongly felt.

The first is that of Oriental poetry—its directness and brevity, its involvement with the life of things, its sense that the poem does not create the poetry but is the revelation of a poetry that is in the world. Here is a poem, "Written on the Wall at Chang's Hermitage," by Tu Fu, a Chinese poet of the eighth century; the translation is by Kenneth Rexroth, who has written excellent nature poems of his own:

It is Spring in the mountains.
I come alone seeking you.
The sound of chopping wood echoes
Between the silent peaks.
The streams are still icy.
There is snow on the trail.
At sunset I reach your grove
In the stony mountain pass.
You want nothing, although at night
You can see the aura of gold
And silver ore all around you.
You have learned to be gentle
As the mountain deer you have tamed.
The way back forgotten, hidden

Away, I become like you,
An empty boat, floating, adrift.

These qualities perhaps reach their height of refine-
ment in haiku, an art that developed both out of and into
a complex awareness of nature:

> I am one
> Who eats his breakfast,
> Gazing at the morning-glories. *Basho*

> Over my legs,
> Stretched out at ease,
> The billowing clouds. *Issa*

> Spring departs,
> Trembling, in the grasses
> Of the fields. *Issa*

"A Haiku," Blyth says, "is not a poem, it is not literature; it is a hand beckoning, a door half-opened, a mirror
wiped clean. It is a way of returning to nature. . . . It is
a way in which the cold winter rain, the swallows of evening, even the very day in its hotness, and the length of
the night become truly alive, share in our humanity,
speak their own silent and expressive language."

The second influence is that of the prose writings of
Henry David Thoreau. In his poems, Thoreau usually
seems weighted and bound by the vagueness and inflated
diction of most romantic nature poetry. It was only in
prose that he could break free into the presence of the
life around him and become a poet. In his prose we see,

maybe for the first time, the poet-as-American, speaking out of the life of an American place—a new place, relatively speaking, the life of which had not been much spoken of by white poets or writers of any kind, and which therefore demanded a clear direct vision. We find this clarity and directness in his prose. We also find a painstaking accuracy of observation, a most unsolemn and refreshing reverence, a sense of being involved in nature, and a rare exuberance and wit. These are samples from his *Journal*:

You tell of active labors, of works of art, and wars the past summer; meanwhile the tortoise eggs underlie this turmoil.

The air over these fields is a foundry full of moulds for casting bluebirds' warbles. Any sound uttered now would take that form. . . .

The fishes are going up the brooks as they open. They are dispersing themselves through the fields and woods, imparting new life into them. They are taking their places under the shelving banks and in the dark swamps. The water running down meets the fishes running up. They hear the latest news. Spring-aroused fishes are running up our veins too.

Now, to give some idea of the contemporary work, I will quote from the three poets I mentioned at the beginning. Very different from each other, they are all alike in seeking a new awareness of nature and their own place in it.

Denise Levertov is a poet deeply interested in myth, as many modern poets have been. With her this is not an antiquarian interest. She has, I think, no wish merely to reconstruct old myths and observances in homage to the past or in opposition to the present; she is interested in them as clues to the meaning and nature of our deepest needs. In her poems, myth never leads inward to a purely imaginative or purely human interior, but outward toward the world. To imagine is to realize, to sense the authentic. The myth is the acceptance and the enactment of the bond between mankind and the world—as in "The Novices," a poem very different from Frost's "Directive," but closely parallel to it:

They enter the bare wood, drawn
by a clear-obscure summons they fear
and have no choice but to heed.

A rustling underfoot, a
long trail to go, the thornbushes grow
across the dwindling paths.

Until the small clearing, where they
anticipate violence, knowing some rite
to be performed, and compelled to it.

The man moves forward, the boy
sees what he means to do: from an oaktree
a chain runs at an angle into earth

and they pit themselves to uproot it,
dogged and frightened, to pull the iron
out of the earth's heart.

But from the further depths of the wood
as they strain and weigh on the great chain
appears the spirit,

the wood-demon who summoned them.
And he is not bestial, not fierce
but an old woodsman,

gnarled, shabby, smelling of smoke and sweat,
of a bear's height and shambling like a bear.
Yet his presence is a spirit's presence

and awe takes their breath.
Gentle and rough, laughing a little,
he makes his will known:

not for an act of force he called them,
for no rite of obscure violence
but that they might look about them

and see intricate branch and bark,
stars of moss and the old scars
left by dead men's saws,

and not ask what the chain was.
To leave the open fields
and enter the forest,

that was the rite.
Knowing there was mystery, they could go.
Go back now! And he receded

among the multitude of forms,
the twists and shadows they saw now, listening
to the hum of the world's wood.

    A. R. Ammons studied science when he was in college,
and his poems have managed to incorporate the view-

point, the curiosity and even the vocabulary of the biologist. He tends to be a poet, not of natural objects, but of natural processes, and so his language seeks to particularize movement and relationship rather than appearance. But if his vision is scientific, it is also mystical: "I admit to mystery / in the obvious. . . ." If he is fascinated by the study of the interweavings of energies into the ecology, he is also fascinated and awe-struck by the unexplainable: "mind rising / from the physical chemistries. . . ." If he finds grounds for affirmation in his comprehension of the world, he finds the possibility of even greater affirmation in the limits of his comprehension: "I know nothing; / still, I cannot help singing. . . ." If all that a man can understand were all there is, if there were no mystery, then the mind would be trapped, and damned within its limits; one should rejoice in understanding, but rejoice also in failing to understand, for in that failure the mind is set free.

Some of Ammons' poems involve an explicit worshipfulness, which consists in the understanding of the failure to understand, the mind's graceful, and grateful, sense of its boundaries:

> I will show you
> the underlying that takes no image to itself,
> cannot be shown or said,
> but weaves in and out of moons and bladderweeds,
> is all and
> beyond destruction
> because created fully in no particular form . . .
>
> ("Identity")

It should be emphasized that the divinity here is sensed as "underlying" rather than overlooking—not the withdrawn author of forms and substances, but one of their properties. His worship is secular, speculative, curious, meditative, studious.

It is one of the obligations of his religious vision to refuse the presumption of the closed forms of a humanistic art. Form, he believes, is in all things, but the forms comprehended in nature or achieved in art are necessarily partial forms, fragments, inferior to the form of the whole creation, which can be neither comprehended nor imagined:

> I see narrow orders, limited tightness, but will
> not run to that easy victory:
> still around the looser, wider forces work:
> I will try
> to fasten into order enlarging grasps of disorder,
> widening
> scope, but enjoying the freedom that
> Scope eludes my grasp, that there is no finality of vision,
> that I have perceived nothing completely
> that tomorrow a new walk is a new walk.
>
> ("Corsons Inlet")

Of these three poets, Gary Snyder is the most austere, the one willing to venture furthest from the human assumptions and enclosures. His poem "Piute Creek" is a spiritual discipline in which he confronts the nonhuman time and space of the Sierra Nevada. His realization of the smallness and shortness of his life in relation to the world's life is of such intensity as to make him virtually

absent from the place and from his own sense of things.
He is present in the poem finally only as another creature, along with moon and rock and juniper and the wild
animals. And in proportion as he withdraws himself and
his human claims, his sense of it grows whole and grand.
He is a worshipper only in the sense that in his clarified
consciousness of it the creation is seen to be awesome
and mysterious, deserving worship:

One granite ridge
A tree, would be enough
Or even a rock, a small creek,
A bark shred in a pool.
Hill beyond hill, folded and twisted
Tough trees crammed
In thin stone fractures
A huge moon on it all, is too much.
The mind wanders. A million
Summers, night air still and the rocks
Warm. Sky over endless mountains.
All the junk that goes with being human
Drops away, hard rock wavers
Even the heavy present seems to fail
This bubble of a heart.
Words and books
Like a small creek off a high ledge
Gone in the dry air.

A clear, attentive mind
Has no meaning but that
Which sees is truly seen.
No one loves rock, yet we are here.

Night chills. A flick
In the moonlight
Slips into Juniper shadow:
Back there unseen
Cold proud eyes
Of Cougar or Coyote
Watch me rise and go.

It is necessary for me to say, ending, that this collection of quotations and comments is not meant to be taken as a definitive statement. Like most things said about poetry by poets, it is personal and somewhat arbitrary. It is an effort to suggest that there is in our poetry an impulse of reverence moving toward the world, toward a new pertinence of speech and a new sense of possibility.

Notes from an Absence
and a Return

(*California*)
Sept. 19, 1968

A dream: Lyndon Johnson, feeling unsafe in the White House because of the discontent of the people, has established himself in an all-glass, bullet- and sound-proof cubicle high over Manhattan Island. On the glass walls he has stuck yellow, red-bordered pennants saying TEXAS. Visited by an association of ministers, he addresses them: "Gentlemen, I believe I may say that I have always been, and still am, a man of frugal cold sweats and funny Bibles."

There seems to me a fundamental distinction between God the Creator and God the Ruler. God the Creator is the God of mystery, a presence felt but not known. God the Ruler is a man-god, limited by (and to) the human understanding. God the Creator rules by creating, by the continuous ramification and metamorphosis of formal energy, as the life forms keep rising out of and falling back into the earth. But God the Ruler rules by decree and by whim, like a tyrant, like the tyrants who invented him. If God rules as Creator, then worship involves the humility of creating, aligning oneself with the creation and drawing on its energy, not the mindless and inert humility of obedience to "revealed" laws.

To be at home in the world, once one has come to the fateful modern consciousness of alternatives, requires a tremendous labor, an endurance of great fear.

Oct. 20

When one lives as a creature within the creation, aligned with it, then one's life passes through the world as a creative force or agent, like a stream of water. Then one can hear "the songs that travel through the air" like the Indians of the Peyote Meeting.

Nov. 17

At dark yesterday I walked home through the golf course at the back of the campus. Enjoyed the marvelous alertness that comes with walking in the dark without a light. All the senses wake up. Hearing is more conscious and acute; peripheral vision becomes a necessary function; there is a complex, delicate *feeling* of the ground one is walking over. The body seems filled out to its limits with an intense consciousness of itself and of things around it. That was the first time I've walked in the dark that way, I think, since we left Kentucky.

It seems to me that I've submitted to the experience of being out here more openly than I expected to. Until recently I was so caught up in my responses to all that is happening here—to what has been happening to *me* here —that it was peculiarly difficult for me to think of what I had left behind. But now I have come deep enough into this experience, sifted and sorted through enough of it, that my mind is quieter. And I have become, in a very cool, knowing way, hungry to be at home again. I want back the clear, exacting sense of myself that I only get from being at work there on my writing and on the place itself. It comes clear that Tanya and I have made a powerful life there, and it is a deep reassurance to feel that power working, holding and drawing me from so far.

Dec. 6

I used to think of meaning as something that one had recourse to—a touchstone or a base. Now it seems to me that unless an act or an occupation is suffused with meaning, constantly and indivisibly meaningful, it is meaningless. It is not possible to work at meaningless work, and then go home or to church or to a museum and experience meaning, as one would recharge a battery. The model would be the life of the primitive hunter or farmer, whose work was never divided from ceremony.

Dec. 11

"If we think of African music as regards intent, we must see . . . that it was a purely *functional* music.

. . . But in the West, the 'triumph of the economic mind over the imaginative,' as Brooks Adams said, made possible this dreadful split between life and art. Hence, a music that is an 'art' music as distinguished from something someone would whistle while tilling a field."

(LeRoi Jones, *Blues People*)

I want, and I think in my farming poems I have been consciously working toward, a poetry that would not be incompatible with barns and gardens and fields and woodlands. The mind, carrying such poetry into such places, would be freed and eased in the presence of *what is there.*

Feb. 18, 1969

The philosophical and also the felt, the nervous, difference between a man moving alone in a landscape and a man moving through the same landscape maintaining an operational relationship to the movements of many other men. The difference between working around our place at Lanes Landing or walking down Camp Branch and driving a freeway or teaching in a university.

It is not the difference between isolation and community. A healthy community would free the man to move alone when he needed to, and it would also inform him, though he moved alone, with adequate principles and ways.

In Faulkner: the sense of oneness with the land, and with the life of the land which informs and transcends physical change, as a force (*the* force?) which can change a man's life. In *Go Down Moses* this results in relinquishment of the white man's superimposed and artificial tenure of the land. To get beyond the mere gesture of relinquishment it is necessary to begin again with the details of the life of a place.

Faulkner, in *The Faulkner-Cowley File*: ". . . maybe a group of Dismal Swamp or Florida Everglades Abolitionists will decide to free the country from machines and will start a movement to do so. . . ." I read that with some feeling of recognition, the sense that this would be one way of stating my own aspiration: to be a Kentucky River Abolitionist, a part of a movement to free the slaves of the machines.

"One must summer and winter with the land and wait its occasions."

(Mary Austin, *The Land of Little Rain*)

March 3

In ten days we leave here to start back to Kentucky. For half a year now we've lived a life radically unlike the life we've chosen and made there at home. What I get from the experience out here is the awareness that the life we want is not merely the one we have chosen and made; it is the one we must be choosing and making. To keep it alive we must be perpetually choosing it and making its differences from among all contrary and alternative possibilities. We must accept the pain and labor of that, or we lose its satisfactions and its joy. Only by risking it, offering it freely to its possibilities, can we keep it.

From Pound, *The Great Digest and the Unwobbling Pivot*:

". . . the real man perfects the nation's culture without leaving his fireside."

"One humane family can humanize a whole state; one courteous family can lift a whole state into courtesy; one grasping and perverse man can drive a nation to chaos."

"Equity is something that springs up from the earth in harmony with earth and with heaven." [Like a plant in a field.]

"Thence the man of breed cannot dodge disciplining himself. Thinking of this self-discipline he cannot fail in good acts toward his relatives; thinking of being good to his blood relatives he cannot skimp his understanding of nature and of mankind; wanting to know mankind he must perforce observe the order of nature and of the heavens."

The thinking of professional reformers and revolutionaries usually fails to escape the machine analogy operative in military and other coercive thinking. They want to organize the people into a human machine. And a machine is by definition subservient to the will of only one man. In the formula "Power to the People" I hear "Power to *me*, who am eager to run the show in the name of the People." The People, of course, are those so designated by their benevolent servant-to-be, who knows so well what is good for them. Thus by diseased speech, politics, as usual, dispenses with the facts.

The Confucian mind escapes the machine analogy by placing the emphasis on specific persons and specific acts. It accepts the discipline of details—which is only to say that it accepts a discipline. What produces the sweat and the results of a real encounter with possibility is details, not slogans.

March 12

Farewell supper at Ed's house with Ed's family and Gurney and Chloe. The gathering charged with the sense that in the half year of being together we have made possibilities that did not exist before, the sense of the life of our community that will survive our separation.

Be joyful because it is humanly possible.

March 14

The relief of mountains and deserts after the overpopulated, overmechanized regions. The oppression of driving mile after mile under a veil of poison. Now it is only in the wild places that a man can sense the rarity of being a man. In the crowded places he is more and more closed in by the feeling that he is ordinary—and that he is, on the average, expendable.

You can best serve civilization by being against what usually passes for it.

(*Kentucky*)
March 24

We've been back home since the night of the eighteenth. This is the first rainy day since we got here. I'm at the Camp with a fire going in the heater. Outside it's 50°, some of the maples and elms are starting to bloom, the river shows the dapplings of muddy water. It has been raining steadily all morning.

When we got here the furnace wasn't working, the toilet wasn't working, the other car and the tiller had to be taken to the garage and started. A lot of little tasks of setting things right and getting started and beginning to live here again. I've pruned the trees and vines in the orchard, gone over the garden once with the tiller, clipped the chickens' wings so they can't fly out of the pen, fixed the furnace and the toilet, etc. And this morning I've swept out the Camp and begun to move my work things back into it.

So here I am again.

March 28

But to be here again is no simple matter. What is inescapable is the complexity of my being here. Most of my friends seem to have the notion that it must be simply a great relief to me to be back on my home ground. Not so. It *is* a relief, certainly—a deep settling of the spirit; I've slept better since I've been back than in all the time I was gone.

But it is other things too. It is not pure or simple, because I am not a tourist here. I have made this place my life. I am its dependent; it is my dependent. And so in addition to the relief and the joy, the profound steady pleasure, of returning, there is a heavy sense of involvement and responsibility. As never before I'm impressed with the dependence of a human place, such as a farm, on human love. After our seven months' absence our place shows clearly its dependence, not so much on the conscious large acts such as a man might do out of duty, but on the hundreds of trivial acts that a man who loves it does every day, without premeditation, in the course of doing other things. The *duties* have all been done; we have nothing to complain about on that score. It is the seven months' absence of our own attentiveness and concern that we continue to notice; its marks are everywhere.

The redeeming aspect of the sense of involvement and responsibility is that it does not stand alone, but is only part of a process, a way of life that includes joy. Not always or necessarily or even preferably the dramatic joy of surprise—though that is one of its possibilities—but the quiet persistent joy of familiarity.

There is also a peculiar hesitance in returning—as there might be in rejoining a deeply loved woman after a long absence. Have I changed? Has the place? Do I still belong here? And then the joy of finding out that I do. I first began to *live* here again when it rained after having been dry; in the relief I felt then, I re-entered the processes of this place, its time and weather. Day before yesterday there was snow. A heavy frost last night. Today is bright and warming.

March 29

In the woods one of the satisfactions is to return to places that are associated with events in my life, that I am bound to by more than familiarity and affection: places I hunted or wandered in when I was a boy, where I have walked and picnicked with Tanya and the children and with friends, where ideas and words have come to me, where I have sat writing, where I have imagined events in my books taking place, where I know some flower will be blooming later in the year. Tanya says one reason we are happy here is that we are learning where to expect things to happen.

At home the great delight is to see the clover and grass now growing on places that were bare when we came. These small healings of the ground are my model accomplishment—everything else I do must aspire to that. While I was at that work the world gained with every move I made, and I harmed nothing.

Our vision of what we wanted here is fleshing itself out. What we have planted is growing. It becomes clearer what must be planted next.

April 2

The big woods. Late afternoon. Cloudy and warm. Has been raining off and on all day. As I came along the creek the crows were ganged up over on the hillside, having found a hawk or an owl.

The old oak stump where I often go to sit is covered with a light green patina of moss now. After the work of insects, woodpeckers, lichens, mosses, fungi, bacteria, by the time a dead tree reaches the ground it has become earth.

I cross over through the woods to the Woodpecker Hollow and sit down. The peepers are going strong in the little wet-weather slue. Doves are calling in the distance. There comes once the brief clear song of a cardinal. Off among the branches I see gray squirrels playing.

A pair of wood ducks comes in on the slue, thirty or forty feet away. They hit the water like precise knife strokes, in a rush. I didn't expect them. A great flash in the nerves. As soon as they have lighted they swim around, the female calling loudly. And then they catch sight of me, some small movement I make, and fly.

A tall water maple, eighteen inches thick, has fallen across the slue since I was here last, a hump of earth turned up with its roots.

A pair of downy woodpeckers arrives at the hollow, clipping to the tree trunks like little brackets, pecking here and there, flying, flirting.

A robin sings strongly off in the woods behind me.

Way off in the back of the woods I occasionally hear one of the pileated woodpeckers.

5:30. I've been here, I guess, a half hour. The flickers begin to arrive for the night. They drum, call outrageously, bow and wobble and display themselves.

Heard singly, the peepers' voices are liquid and fluty. Together they make a sound that is utterly surrounding and inundating. It fills and echoes in the head so that the ears seem to yell back.

I can hear one of the pileateds drumming. A brief roll, building heavily and dwindling.

5:50. A pileated had come to a tree nearby, but I didn't see him until he flew. For all the boldness and grandeur in the presence and movements of these birds, they have a furtiveness about them. They are timid and can skulk around like spies. Long before they finally fly into the hollow for the night, in that swooping, always breathtaking entrance, one is conscious of them hovering about in the distance, silent and fluttery-seeming as moths at a window.

With the scar of the new road on one side, and on another the huge scrape where they took up dirt for the fill, the life and meaning of this place are more poignant than ever. The little branch now flows over the yellow silt of eroded subsoil. One feels that every natural place now stands under the heavy syllable WHEN?

Something keeps wrinkling the edge of the water. My legs are beginning to go to sleep, so I get up and walk down to see. The peepers all hush at once. Among the dead leaves under the water I see a small salamander. There is a gelatin ball of eggs fastened to a weed stem. Also a few water striders.

I draw back from the edge of the water and squat down in a little patch of cane. About 6:30 a pileated clips itself to a tall slender sycamore and almost at once disappears into a hole. Then two more come, more boldly, the white of their wings flashing in the dusk, and I hear the sounds their wings make, whipping and chuffing as they turn, almost like somebody shaking a throw rug or a pillow slip. I watch one of these go to roost. He stands braced on his tail at the lip of the hole for some time, leaning to look in and then rearing back to look around outside. It is as though they study the difference between the light outside and the dark inside, and will go in for the night only when the difference has grown exactly small enough. I have seen hens behave much the same way going into the hen house to roost. Finally he goes in, and turns and looks out for a few seconds, and then withdraws for the night.

April 13

Phlox, trout lily, poppy, crinkleroot, spring beauty, bloodroot, violets, rue anemone, Dutchman's breeches, bluebell. All those in bloom. And mayapple, hound's tongue, larkspur, columbine, all coming on. The woods floor reminds me now of the foreground of Botticelli's *Spring*. One walks in the crisis of the fear of trampling something exquisitely formed. But also with the sense, joyful if anything is, of time passing beautifully, of time passing *through* beauty, fulfilled in it in degree and detail beyond calculation, and so not wasted or lost. In the woods, as in the place of a skilled and loving workman, time departs free and unburdened from the past. Walking among all these flowers, I cannot *see* enough. One is aware of the abundance of lovely things—forms, scents, colors—lavished on the earth beyond any human capacity to perceive or number or imitate. And aware of the economy, the modest principle of the building earth under the dead leaves, by which such abundance is assured.

This is the enemy in man's "war against nature."

All these places of unforced loveliness, whose details keep touching in my mind the memory of great paintings, now lie within the sound of the approach of an alien army whose bulldozers fly the flag of the American economy (hardly the economy of the topsoil). This country is an unknown place suffering the invasion of a people whose minds have never touched the earth.

As I left the house I saw a yellow-throated warbler in an elm near the barn, and then another at the Three Streams. At the top of the ridge I watched a pair of red-tailed hawks soaring on the rising air currents above the bluffs. They moved in the broad loops of a spiral which slowly advanced above the tilt of the woods. As they turned, the one on the outside veered to the inside, and as they came around again, the one now on the outside veered to the inside. They repeated this over and over. The movement was very dancelike and graceful. It would be impossible, I would guess, to diagram it intelligibly, but free in the sky, leaving no marks, the pattern was clear and simple and coherent. Later I saw one of the pair hunting, circling and screaming, low to the treetops—a very different sort of flight, agitated and urgent. And still later one of them was being bullied by crows on the north slope along Camp Branch.

I come more and more to look on each creature as living and moving always at the center—one of the infinite number of centers—of an arrangement of processes that reaches through the universe. The interlocking lives of the creatures, like a coat of chain mail, by which the creation saves itself from death.

I went across the wooded points above the river and Cane Run and Camp Branch, in and out of the draws, and then down to Camp Branch, and up to the old barn, and up the wagon road, and over the ridge, and down the old landing road, and across the hollow into the pasture behind the house.

This Port Royal, this state of Kentucky, these United States, in which everything is supposedly named and numbered and priced, are unlikely to know what lies out of sight of the paved roads. I walk often through places unknown by any name or fact or event to people who live almost within calling distance of them, yet more worthy of their interest, I think, than the distant places to which they devote so much of their attention. If we were a truly civilized and indigenous people such places would be named for what is characteristic of them, they would be known and talked about, people would visit them as they now visit places of commercial entertainment, as familiarly as they visit their friends. People would walk carefully and attentively and reverently in them. There would be a lore about them that each generation would both inherit and add to. Knowledge of them would pass intimately through families and friendships. The country would be full of such places, each known and visited only by a few. The human value of the land would then come to be what humans *knew* about it, and wealth would no longer prey on it.

On my walk I carried a 15 × lens. Looked at through it, the bluebells are depthless; you seem to be looking deep in or far out. Like looking down into clear, still, blue water, or off a mountaintop into the sky.

After we planted garden last Tuesday Tanya spoke of how much she liked the idea that we had done it, not because of any convention or custom or law, but because it was *time*.

April 25

A light frost last night. Mist from the river kept it off the fruit trees.

The morning sunny. I left the house after breakfast, and walked up the branch and over the hill.

Sitting on a log near the top of the bluebell slope. The woods leafing out. Around me the birds are singing, and in a larger circle I hear the farmers' tractors getting on with the spring work.

May 21

If you aren't for us you're against us, somebody is always saying. That seems to me a sad little pair of options, insofar as to any kind of intelligence the possibilities ought to be numerous, if not infinite. Intelligence *consists* in being for and against such things as political movements *up to a point*, which it is the task of intelligence to define. In my judgment intelligence never goes whole hog for anything public, especially political movements. Across the whole range of politics now (and I suppose always) you find people willing to act on the assumption that there is some simple abstraction that will explain and solve the problems of the world, and who go direct from the discovery of the abstraction to the forming of an organization to promote it. In my opinion those people are all about equally dangerous, and I don't believe anything they say. What I hold out for is the possibility that a man can live decently *without* knowing all the answers, or believing that he does—can live decently even in the understanding that life is unspeakably complex and unspeakably subtle in its complexity. The decency, I think, would be in acting out of the awareness that personal acts of compassion, love, humility, honesty are better, and more adequate, responses to that complexity than any public abstraction or theory or organization. What is wrong with our cities—and I don't see how you can have a great civilization without great cities—may be that the mode of life in them has become almost inescapably organizational.

It used to be that every time I heard of some public action somewhere to promote some cause I believed in, I would be full of guilt because I wasn't there. If they were marching in Washington to protest the war, and if I deplored the war, then how could my absence from Washington be anything but a sin? That was the organizational protestant conscience: in order to believe in my virtue I needed some organization to pat me on the head and tell me I was virtuous. But if I can't promote what I hope for in Port Royal, Ky., then why go to Washington to promote it?

What succeeds in Port Royal succeeds in the world.

June 29

This place has become the form of my work, its discipline, in the same way the sonnet has been the form and discipline of the work of other poets: if it doesn't fit it's not true.

Oct. 25

The work of the growing season is nearly finished. The raspberry bed is mulched. The rye is up in the garden. Last week I cut down a lot of the trees in the big slip in the riverbank. I cut them three or four feet from the ground and only part way through, leaving them attached to the stumps, and letting them fall crisscrossed. They make a kind of loose thatch over the slip. The idea is that they will slow the current when the river is high, and allow the silt to fill the cavity in the bank.

Probably because of the order and rest that this fall work settles into, I've begun to recover a harmony with the seasonal motions and demands of this place. The long stay in California last fall and winter broke this harmony, and I had no way to realize how thoroughly I had lost it until now, when it has begun to come back. That accounts for much of the clumsiness and behindhandedness I felt in the summer's work—work that needed to have been prepared for last fall and winter when I wasn't here. And the connections between times, and between time and work, are so subtle that I apparently have to be here to do the work before I can know what work must be done. I didn't realize what work had been left out last fall until I began to do it *this* fall. In the work is where my relation to this place comes alive. The real knowledge survives in the work, not in the memory. To love this place and hold out for its meanings and keep its memories, without undertaking any of its work, would be to falsify it.

Oct. 26

In the last few months I have had to consider more openly than before that our use of our place is in some ways still far from a success. Out of a history so much ruled by the motto Think Big, we have come to a place and a need that require us to learn to think little. Instead of ostentation we have undertaken modesty; instead of haste, patience; for the discipline of generalizations we have begun to substitute the discipline of details. When we came here, what I knew of farming had been learned on farms of several hundred acres of good land; and we have begun here at a time when the trend is toward ever larger and more specialized operations, and when smaller farmers are giving up or being forced out—when, in short, the skills and the economics of the small holding have been badly weakened. In undertaking to build some sort of integrated family economy on a few acres, mostly steep and mostly neglected, there has been for those reasons and others a good deal of awkwardness and a lot of waste—of effort and time and money. We have invested in the wrong tools and the wrong projects, have become ensnarled in bad plans, have been too slow to recognize the obvious. That is, we often have, not always. But by this awkwardness and this partial success we can see that we have not got to where we are by anything so simple as deciding what we wanted to do and then doing it—as if we had shopped in a display of lives and selected one. We have, instead, in the midst of living, and with time passing, been discovering how we want to live, and inventing the ways.

Oct. 28

When we woke up this morning there was a heavy frost and a thick fog. Before sunup everything was furred with ice, dull gray, and the fog shut off the distances. And then the sun came through—the sudden difference of throwing a bucket of water on sunlit boards. The white frost gleams on everything. Strands of spiderweb looped along tree limbs and fences are thick as trot line, and brilliant. As the day warms it is windless and still, the leaves coming down steady as rain, falling of their own weight. With the sun on it, the tin roof begins to click, warming up.

I haven't been conscious before of how invariably when I have sensed or imagined the life of another creature, a tree or bird or an animal, I have had to begin by imagining my own absence—as though there was a necessary competition between my life and theirs. I looked upon my ability to imagine myself absent as a virtue. It seems to me now that it was an evasion. I began this morning to feel something truer—the beginning of the knowledge that the other creatures and I are here together.

For years the burden of my work has been the sense of being implicated, by inheritance and by various failures of consciousness of my own, in a phase of history that is malignant. Now what I am suddenly aware of is the possibility—or the hope?—of passing beyond guilt, which is clearly the source of my obsession with the absence metaphor.

The old sycamore down in the corner of the bottom— that survived the ice jam of 1918, that was alive when my grandfathers were boys—*and I* are alive now, this morning, while the spiderwebs are visible with ice and light, and the leaves are falling. We are moving in a relationship, a design, that is definite—though shadowy to me— like people in a dance.

A Homage to Dr. Williams

I have always been attracted to the work of William Carlos Williams because of his use of the art of writing as an instrument by which a man may arrive in his place and maintain himself there. I am still involved in comprehending the implications of such a labor, but this has been the fascination and the solace I have found in him from the first. He has always about him the excitement of the awareness that poetry, as much as the axe or the plow, is a necessity of discovery and settlement, and of the husbanding and neighboring that must follow.

His poems and stories and essays record the lifelong practice of citizenship, the unceasing labor of keeping responsibly conscious of where he was. He knew, as few white Americans have ever known, that a man has not meaningfully arrived in his place in body until he has arrived in spirit as well, and that the consummation of arrival is identification:

Say it! No ideas but in things. Mr.
Paterson has gone away
to rest and write. Inside the bus one sees
his thoughts sitting and standing. His
thoughts alight and scatter. . . .

(*Paterson*, Book One)

What he accomplished was a sustained and intricate act of patriotism in the largest sense of that word—a thousand times more precise and loving and preserving than any patriotism ever contemplated by officials of the government or leaders of parties.

At times the usefulness of his work has been made so vivid to me that what I know of him has become part of what I know of myself. One such time was an overcast day late in the summer of 1962. I was riding a bus out of New York City across the marshes and the industrial suburbs of New Jersey. That fall I was to take a job in New York, and I was hunting a place to live. I was between places, uprooted, alien in that place, deeply depressed. And then I suddenly thought of Williams—all those lovely poems that had grown out of and so heartily savored the life of such places as I saw—and I felt wonderfully comforted and relieved. Life was possible there after all! I had known it for years! And though I never found a place to live in New Jersey, Williams' poems have helped to satisfy me of the possibility of life wherever I have lived. It occurs to me now that no more could be asked of a poet. No more could be asked of a man.

The necessity, the *usefulness*, of poetry! Williams was certain of it. Man cannot live by bread alone, and Williams' work is full of the assurance that he is providing us the staff of life. In the great love poem of his last years, "Asphodel, that Greeny Flower," as in other poems, he speaks directly of it:

> Look at
> what passes for the new.
> You will not find it there but in
> despised poems.
> It is difficult
> to get the news from poems
> yet men die miserably every day
> for lack
> of what is to be found there.

A poem was never, for him, merely an object of art; it was not a specialist's product. He spoke of poetry as the life force, not a "creative act" but one of the acts of the creation, a part of the sum of

> All that which makes the pear ripen
> or the poet's line
> come true!
>
> ("Deep Religious Faith")

It is the power by which a man gifted and trained in verse might find speech and so, in his way, clarify himself and his neighborhood.

In his poems he did not speak as a poet but as a man.

Having come up under the influence of the more superficial techniques of "explication," which encouraged us to read everything as if it were an exercise, I was slow to recognize this. Having learned to think of him as a poet in the specialist sense, I was slow to see him; in "The Host" for instance, a man speaking in worship:

There is nothing to eat,
      seek it where you will,
            but of the body of the Lord.
The blessed plants
      and the sea, yield it
            to the imagination
intact.

While the experts haggle whether God is dead, as if that could be settled by somebody's argument, here is something of the life of God where none of them have yet suspected it: in the world, in a poet's book.

In the same way I was slow to see anything political in Williams. And yet he is full of concern for politics, for matters important to the community of us. But he does not speak as a politician. He could not quit being a poet in order to become political any more than he could quit being a man in order to become a poet. One thinks of the effort he made toward the end of his life to speak of the bomb, to contain it in an order of comprehension, as though in answer to a feeling of community obligation. Or there is the brilliant anger of the poem "To Elsie" in *Spring and All*, in which his concern for women and their fate offers a profound political measure:

> young slatterns, bathed
> ın filth
> from Monday to Saturday
>
> to be tricked out that night
> with gauds
> from imaginations which have no
>
> peasant traditions to give them
> character

And he goes on to speak of a servant girl, Elsie, whose voluptuous ungainly body was

> addressed to cheap
> jewelry
> and rich young men with fine eyes
>
> as if the earth under our feet
> were
> an excrement of some sky
>
> and we degraded prisoners
> destined
> to hunger until we eat filth

Is that political poetry? As I care to use the adjective, it is. It would be perfectly useless and bewildering, perhaps, to the average politician, a political specialist. But how serviceable and clarifying it is, once we have set aside the current abstractions and categories of politics. The poem is telling us precisely what is wrong with us.

And yet, because of the exacting energy of its love for the girl and its grief over her, it simply *cannot* produce a high-toned political abstraction or slogan. By its nature it is a world apart from the dumbfounding earth-polluting blither (The Great Society, The Great Leap Forward) characteristic of government talk from here to China. It fulfills itself in its facts, and does not rant or pontificate. It is preceded by a poem about "Banjo jazz" and is followed by one about lilacs. And far indeed from any political fashion that I know is his assertion—that I believe to be entirely correct—of the importance of peasant traditions.

The speech of politicians, political rhetoric, grows out of the pretense that the politician is not a man, but is somehow infallible. This sort of speech, no matter whose it is, is preparing the world to fight—to the last man—the final war. The poetry that is most useful to us, that has most devotedly sought the humble exactitude of the personal, never makes the deathly pretense of being more than human, and if we will read it, it will help to keep us from making such a pretense. What Williams exemplifies is that a man is most a poet—and, hard as it may be for us to believe it, most a citizen—when he is most humanely and exactingly a man. The measure that so obsessed him, the form and energy of the poetic line, what is it but the obligation and the distinction of a responsible manliness?

Looking back recently through some of his poems, I have been impressed again by the way certain passages I never particularly noticed before suddenly stand out, epigraphs for some new awareness I have come to, some new whereabouts of my concern. His work seems to keep ahead of me, like a man's shadow when he walks eastward in the afternoon, and I have the comfort of believing that I will not exhaust the delight I take in it.

The Regional Motive

In thinking about myself as a writer whose work and whose life have been largely formed in relation to one place, I am often in the neighborhood of the word "regional." And almost as often as I get into its neighborhood I find that the term very quickly becomes either an embarrassment or an obstruction. For I do not know any word that is more sloppily defined in its usage, or more casually understood.

There is, for instance, a "regionalism" based upon pride, which behaves like nationalism. And there is a "regionalism" based upon condescension, which specializes in the quaint and the eccentric and the picturesque, and which behaves in general like an exploitive industry. These varieties, and their kindred, have in common a dependence on false mythology that tends to generalize and stereotype the life of a region. That is to say it tends to impose false literary or cultural generalizations upon false geographical generalizations.

The evils of such generalizations are abundantly exemplified by the cult of "the South." I take for instance the following sentences from John W. Corrington and Miller Williams' Introduction to their anthology, *Southern Writing in the Sixties*:

The landscape of the South that is most haunted is within the Southern man. And there, too, the ghosts have names. They have been named before, and the names are not ours, but they are good and honest names. They are Religion and History, Place and Responsibility.

The tone of spurious piety here, the accrediting to one place of virtues it can only have in common with many other places and other people, the melodrama of referring to concepts as "ghosts," all strike me as typical of what is false and destructive in the conventions of Southern regionalism. Are the editors, one would like to know, talking about George Wallace or Martin Luther King? Do the concepts propounded here as literary virtues apply to Homer and Dante and Thoreau less than to Allen Tate? With that sentence about "Religion and History, Place and Responsibility" we are supposedly ascending into the highest reaches of human experience; in reality, however, the direction is toward the obscuring chauvinisms of Southern Hospitality and Southern Fried Chicken.

In writing and criticism the effect of such talk and such thinking is to transform myth into fantasy. Morally, it functions as a distraction from the particular realities and needs of particular places. A believer in Southern Responsibility, as somehow a unique regional inheritance, will be slow to see that in the South responsibility, like hospitality, has often been too exclusive to deserve the name. Thus generalized, regional pieties blind a man to his whereabouts and his condition. Like the abstractions of Economics and Heaven and Progress, they come between him and his place and cause him to be, not its steward and preserver, but its destroyer. Or they facilitate his utter detachment from his native place and condition. "The mind of the South," for instance, can be transported to comfortable chairs of literature in Northern universities, whereas the *land* of the South, as Faulkner well knew, can be dealt with only at home and in the particularity of personal dedication and personal behavior.

Further on in their Introduction, Corrington and Williams provide a most revealing example of the moral distortion of exploitive or sentimental regionalism. "The land," they write, "is scarred by [history] and the grass is greener for what the land holds." Here the chauvinism of the earlier quote has reached the ground, and is revealed as nonsense. For it is obvious that on land scarred by history the grass cannot be greener, not even *figuratively* greener. The first part of the sentence is perfectly correct: the land of the South, like that of the North and the West, has been scarred by history; indeed the history of the white man's life on this continent has been to an alarming extent the history of the waste and exhaustion and degradation of the land. But the second half of the sentence reveals a disastrous moral confusion: Shall we heal those scars by the establishment of a decent and preserving community, aware of its complex dependence on and obligation to the land, or shall we enshrine the scars and preserve *them* as monuments to the so-called glories of our history?

The health and even the continuance of our life in America, in all regions, require that we enact in the most particular terms a responsible relationship to the land. For that reason the agrarianism of the Southern Agrarians was, in my opinion, a beginning that promised something in the way of a cure. But the withdrawal of the most gifted of those people into the Northern colleges and universities invalidated their thinking, and reduced their effort to the level of an academic exercise. And I suspect that their withdrawal was facilitated by a tendency to love the land, not for its life, but for its historical associations—that is, their agrarianism was doomed to remain theoretical by a sentimental faith that history makes the grass green whether the land is well farmed or not.*

---

* Though I would think it dishonest to alter this and the earlier reference to "comfortable chairs of literature in Northern universities" in such a way as to imply that I never wrote them as first published, I feel nevertheless that certain qualifications are in order. In the first place, it would have been no more than appropriate to assume that there were compelling personal reasons, unknown to me, for the departure of the Agrarians from their region. In the second place, it is ungrateful and inaccurate to imply that their thinking has been without effect. I am uncertain what the *general* effect has been, but it is obvious, I trust, that the effect *on me* has been large. My proper con-

The regional motive is false when the myths and abstractions of a place are valued apart from the place itself; that is regionalism as nationalism. It is also false when the region is made the standard of its own experience—when, that is, perspective is narrowed by condescension or pride so that a man is unable to bring to bear on the life of his place as much as he is able to know. That is exploitive regionalism. If they had written under its standard Faulkner would have had to disavow that part of his mind that knew the "Ode on a Grecian Urn"; Thoreau's knowledge of the Orient would have been a mere flourish, not useful; William Carlos Williams would have had to shrug off the influence of Villon and Chaucer and Fabre.

The regionalism that I adhere to could be defined simply as *local life aware of itself*. It would tend to substitute for the myths and stereotypes of a region a particular knowledge of the life of the *place* one lives in and intends to *continue* to live in. It pertains to living as much as to writing, and it pertains to living *before* it pertains to writing. The motive of such regionalism is the awareness that local life is intricately dependent, for its quality but also for its continuance, upon local knowledge.

Some useful insights into the nature and the value of the sort of regionalism I am talking about can be found in the work of Thomas Hardy. In *The Woodlanders*,

---

cern, then, is not to complain against the departure of the Agrarians, but to warn that their departure should not be taken either as disproof of the validity of their principles, or as justification of absentee regionalism (agrarianism without agriculture).

comparing Dr. Fitzpiers' relation to Little Hintock with that of the natives, Hardy writes:

Winter in a solitary house in the country, without society, is tolerable, nay, even enjoyable and delightful, given . . . old association—an almost exhaustive biographical or historical acquaintance with every object . . . within the observer's horizon.

And he goes on to say that even though a place "may have beauty, grandeur, salubrity, convenience," it still cannot be comfortably inhabited by people "if it lack memories." And in a letter to H. Rider Haggard about the effects of the migration of the English working people, Hardy wrote that, "there being no continuity of environment in their lives, there is no continuity of information, the names, stories, and relics of one place being speedily forgotten under the incoming facts of the next."

From the perspective of the environmental crisis of our own time, I think we have to add to Hardy's remarks a further realization: if the land is made fit for human habitation by memory and "old association," it is also true that by memory and association men are made fit to inhabit the land. At present our society is almost entirely nomadic, without the comfort or the discipline of such memories, and it is moving about on the face of this continent with a mindless destructiveness, of substance and of meaning and of value, that makes Sherman's march to the sea look like a prank.

Without a complex knowledge of one's place, and without the faithfulness to one's place on which such knowledge depends, it is inevitable that the place will be used carelessly, and eventually destroyed. Without such knowledge and faithfulness, moreover, the culture of a country will be superficial and decorative, functional only insofar as it may be a symbol of prestige, the affectation of an elite or "in" group. And so I look upon the sort of regionalism that I am talking about not just as a recurrent literary phenomenon, but as a necessity of civilization and of survival.

I notice a prevalent tendency among my contemporaries to think of existing conditions as if they were not only undeniable, but unassailable as well, as if the highest use of intelligence were not the implementation of vision but merely the arrangement of a cheap settlement. It would appear that any fact, by virtue of being a fact, must somehow be elevated to the status of Eternal Truth. Thus if we have become a nation of urban nomads, at the expense of human society and at the world's expense, the common anticipation seems to be that, knocking around in this way, we will sooner or later evolve an urban nomadic civilization that will correct the present destructiveness of urban nomadism. I do not believe it. I do not believe it even though I am sure that my disbelief will be thought by many people to be impractical and unrealistic. I certainly am aware that there have been great nomadic civilizations. But it seems to me that those were evolved in response to natural conditions of climate and soil, whereas *our* nomadic civilization has evolved in response to an economy that is based upon a deliberate wastefulness. That a desert should produce a nomadic life is perfectly understandable. That my own section of Kentucky—well wooded, well watered, having had originally the best of soils, and still abundantly fertile—should have produced a race of nomads is simply preposterous. It could have happened only by a series of monumental errors—in land use, in economics, in intellectual fashion.

With the urbanization of the country so nearly complete, it may seem futile to the point of madness to pursue an ethic and a way of life based upon devotion to a place and devotion to the land. And yet I do pursue such an ethic and such a way of life, for I believe they hold the only possibility, not just for a decent life, but for survival. And the two concerns—decency and survival—are *not* separate, but are intimately related. For, as the history of agriculture in the Orient very strongly suggests, it is not the life that is fittest (by which we have meant the most violent) that survives, but rather the life that is most decent—the life that is most generous and wise in its relation to the earth.

Think Little

First there was Civil Rights, and then there was the War, and now it is the Environment. The first two of this sequence of causes have already risen to the top of the nation's consciousness and declined somewhat in a remarkably short time. I mention this in order to begin with what I believe to be a justifiable skepticism. For it seems to me that the Civil Rights Movement and the Peace Movement, as popular causes in the electronic age, have partaken far too much of the nature of fads. Not for all, certainly, but for too many they have been the fashionable politics of the moment. As causes they have been undertaken too much in ignorance; they have been too much simplified; they have been powered too much by impatience and guilt of conscience and short-term enthusiasm, and too little by an authentic social vision and long-term conviction and deliberation. For most people those causes have remained almost entirely abstract; there has been too little personal involvement, and too much involvement in organizations that were insisting that *other* organizations should do what was right.

There is considerable danger that the Environment Movement will have the same nature: that it will be a public cause, served by organizations that will self-righteously criticize and condemn other organizations, inflated for a while by a lot of public talk in the media, only to be replaced in its turn by another fashionable crisis. I hope that will not happen, and I believe that there are ways to keep it from happening, but I know that if this effort is carried on solely as a public cause, if millions of people cannot or will not undertake it as a *private* cause as well, then it is *sure* to happen. In five years the energy of our present concern will have petered out in a series of public gestures—and no doubt in a series of empty laws—and a great, and perhaps the last, human opportunity will have been lost.

It need not be that way. A better possibility is that the movement to preserve the environment will be seen to be, as I think it has to be, not a digression from the civil rights and peace movements, but the logical culmination of those movements. For I believe that the separation of these three problems is artificial. They have the same cause, and that is the mentality of greed and exploitation. The mentality that exploits and destroys the natural environment is the same that abuses racial and economic minorities, that imposes on young men the tyranny of the military draft, that makes war against peasants and women and children with the indifference of technology. The mentality that destroys a watershed and then panics at the threat of flood is the same mentality that gives institutionalized insult to black people and then panics at the prospect of race riots. It is the same mentality that can mount deliberate warfare against a civilian population and then express moral shock at the logical consequence of such warfare at My Lai. We would be fools to believe that we could solve any one of these problems without solving the others.

To me, one of the most important aspects of the environmental movement is that it brings us not just to another public crisis, but to a crisis of the protest movement itself. For the environmental crisis should make it dramatically clear, as perhaps it has not always been before, that there is no public crisis that is not also private. To most advocates of civil rights, racism has seemed mostly the fault of someone else. For most advocates of peace the war has been a remote reality, and the burden of the blame has seemed to rest mostly on the government. I am certain that these crises have been more private, and that we have each suffered more from them and been more responsible for them, than has been readily apparent, but the connections have been difficult to see. Racism and militarism have been institutionalized among us for too long for our personal involvement in those evils to be easily apparent to us. Think, for example, of all the Northerners who assumed—until black people attempted to move into *their* neighborhoods—that racism was a Southern phenomenon. And think how quickly—one might almost say how naturally—among some of its members the peace movement has spawned policies of deliberate provocation and violence.

But the environmental crisis rises closer to home. Every time we draw a breath, every time we drink a glass of water, every time we eat a bite of food we are suffering from it. And more important, every time we indulge in, or depend on, the wastefulness of our economy—and our economy's first principle is waste—we are *causing* the crisis. Nearly every one of us, nearly every day of his life, is contributing *directly* to the ruin of this planet. A protest meeting on the issue of environmental abuse is not a convocation of accusers, it is a convocation of the guilty. That realization ought to clear the smog of self-righteousness that has almost conventionally hovered over these occasions, and let us see the work that is to be done.

In this crisis it is certain that every one of us has a public responsibility. We must not cease to bother the government and the other institutions to see that they never become comfortable with easy promises. For myself, I want to say that I hope never again to go to Frankfort to present a petition to the governor on an issue so vital as that of strip mining, only to be dealt with by some ignorant functionary—as several of us were not so long ago, the governor himself being "too busy" to receive us. Next time I will go prepared to wait as long as necessary to see that the petitioners' complaints and their arguments are heard *fully*—and by the governor. And then I will hope to find ways to keep those complaints and arguments from being forgotten until something is done to relieve them. The time is past when it was enough merely to elect our officials. We will have to elect them and then go and *watch* them and keep our hands on them, the way the coal companies do. We have made a tradition in Kentucky of putting self-servers, and worse, in charge of our vital interests. I am sick of it. And I think that one way to change it is to make Frankfort a less comfortable place. I believe in American political principles, and I will not sit idly by and see those principles destroyed by sorry practice. I am ashamed and deeply distressed that American government should have become the chief cause of disillusionment with American principles.

And so when the government in Frankfort again proves too stupid or too blind or too corrupt to see the plain truth and to act with simple decency, I intend to be there, and I trust that I won't be alone. I hope, moreover, to be there, not with a sign or a slogan or a button, but with the facts and the arguments. A crowd whose discontent has risen no higher than the level of slogans is *only* a crowd. But a crowd that understands the reasons for its discontent and knows the remedies is a vital community, and it will have to be reckoned with. I would rather go before the government with two men who have a competent understanding of an issue, and who therefore deserve a hearing, than with two thousand who are vaguely dissatisfied.

But even the most articulate public protest is not enough. We don't live in the government or in institutions or in our public utterances and acts, and the environmental crisis has its roots in our *lives*. By the same token, environmental health will also be rooted in our lives. That is, I take it, simply a fact, and in the light of it we can see how superficial and foolish we would be to think that we could correct what is wrong merely by tinkering with the institutional machinery. The changes that are required are fundamental changes in the way we are living.

What we are up against in this country, in any attempt to invoke private responsibility, is that we have nearly destroyed private life. Our people have given up their independence in return for the cheap seductions and the shoddy merchandise of so-called "affluence." We have delegated all our vital functions and responsibilities to salesmen and agents and bureaus and experts of all sorts. We cannot feed or clothe ourselves, or entertain ourselves, or communicate with each other, or be charitable or neighborly or loving, or even respect ourselves, without recourse to a merchant or a corporation or a public-service organization or an agency of the government or a style-setter or an expert. Most of us cannot think of dissenting from the opinions or the actions of one organization without first forming a new organization. Individualism is going around these days in uniform, handing out the party line on individualism. Dissenters want to publish their personal opinions over a thousand signatures.

. The Confucian *Great Digest* says that the "chief way for the production of wealth" (and he is talking about real goods, not money) is "that the producers be many and that the mere consumers be few. . . ." But even in the much-publicized rebellion of the young against the materialism of the affluent society, the consumer mentality is too often still intact: the standards of behavior are still those of kind and quantity, the security sought is still the security of numbers, and the chief motive is still the consumer's anxiety that he is missing out on what is "in." In this state of total consumerism— which is to say a state of helpless dependence on things and services and ideas and motives that we have forgotten how to provide ourselves—all meaningful contact between ourselves and the earth is broken. We do not understand the earth in terms either of what it offers us or of what it requires of us, and I think it is the rule that people inevitably destroy what they do not understand. Most of us are not directly responsible for strip mining and extractive agriculture and other forms of environmental abuse. But we are guilty nevertheless, for we connive in them by our ignorance. We are ignorantly dependent on them. We do not know enough about them; we do not have a particular enough sense of their danger. Most of us, for example, not only do not know how to produce the best food in the best way—we don't know how to produce any kind in any way. Our model citizen is a sophisticate who before puberty understands how to produce a baby, but who at the age of thirty will not know how to produce a potato. And for this condition we have elaborate rationalizations, instructing us that dependence for everything on somebody else is efficient and economical and a scientific miracle. I say, instead, that it is madness, mass produced. A man who understands the weather only in terms of golf is participating in a chronic public insanity that either he or his descendants will be bound to realize as suffering. I believe that the death of the world is breeding in such minds much more certainly and much faster than in any political capital or atomic arsenal.

For an index of our loss of contact with the earth we need only look at the condition of the American farmer —who must in our society, as in every society, enact man's dependence on the land, and his responsibility to it. In an age of unparalleled affluence and leisure, the American farmer is harder pressed and harder worked than ever before; his margin of profit is small, his hours are long; his outlays for land and equipment and the expenses of maintenance and operation are growing rapidly greater; he cannot compete with industry for labor; he is being forced more and more to depend on the use of destructive chemicals and on the wasteful methods of haste and anxiety. As a class, farmers are one of the despised minorities. So far as I can see, farming is considered marginal or incidental to the economy of the country, and farmers, when they are thought of at all, are thought of as hicks and yokels, whose lives do not fit into the modern scene. The average American farmer is now an old man whose sons have moved away to the cities. His knowledge, and his intimate connection with the land, are about to be lost. The small independent farmer is going the way of the small independent craftsmen and storekeepers. He is being forced off the land into the cities, his place taken by absentee owners, corporations, and machines. Some would justify all this in the name of efficiency. As I see it, it is an enormous social and economic and cultural blunder. For the small farmers who lived on their farms *cared* about their land. And given their established connection to their land—which was often hereditary and traditional as well as economic—they could have been encouraged to care for it more competently than they have so far. The corporations and machines that replace them will never be bound to the land by the sense of birthright and continuity, or by the love that enforces care. They will be bound by the rule of efficiency, which takes thought only of the volume of the year's produce, and takes no thought of the slow increment of the life of the land, not measurable in pounds or dollars, which will assure the livelihood and the health of the coming generations.

If we are to hope to correct our abuses of each other and of other races and of our land, and if our effort to correct these abuses is to be more than a political fad that will in the long run be only another form of abuse, then we are going to have to go far beyond public protest and political action. We are going to have to rebuild the substance and the integrity of private life in this country. We are going to have to gather up the fragments of knowledge and responsibility that we have parceled out to the bureaus and the corporations and the specialists, and we are going to have to put those fragments back together again in our own minds and in our families and households and neighborhoods. We need better government, no doubt about it. But we also need better minds, better friendships, better marriages, better communities.

We need persons and households that do not have to wait upon organizations, but can make necessary changes in themselves, on their own.

For most of the history of this country our motto, implied or spoken, has been Think Big. I have come to believe that a better motto, and an essential one now, is Think Little. That implies the necessary change of thinking and feeling, and suggests the necessary work. Thinking Big has led us to the two biggest and cheapest political dodges of our time: plan-making and law-making. The lotus-eaters of this era are in Washington, D.C., Thinking Big. Somebody comes up with a problem, and somebody in the government comes up with a plan or a law. The result, mostly, has been the persistence of the problem, and the enlargement and enrichment of the government.

But the discipline of thought is not generalization; it is detail, and it is personal behavior. While the government is "studying" and funding and organizing its Big Thought, nothing is being done. But the citizen who is willing to Think Little, and, accepting the discipline of that, to go ahead on his own, is already solving the problem. A man who is trying to live as a neighbor to his neighbors will have a lively and practical understanding of the work of peace and brotherhood, and let there be no mistake about it—he is *doing* that work. A couple who make a good marriage, and raise healthy, morally competent children, are serving the world's future more directly and surely than any political leader, though they never utter a public word. A good farmer who is dealing with the problem of soil erosion on an acre of ground has a sounder grasp of that problem and *cares* more about it and is probably doing more to solve it than any bureaucrat who is talking about it in general. A man who is willing to undertake the discipline and the difficulty of mending his own ways is worth more to the conservation movement than a hundred who are insisting merely that the government and the industries mend *their* ways.

If you are concerned about the proliferation of trash, then by all means start an organization in your community to do something about it. But before—*and while*—you organize, pick up some cans and bottles yourself. That way, at least, you will assure yourself and others that you mean what you say. If you are concerned about air pollution, help push for government controls, but drive your car less, use less fuel in your home. If you are worried about the damming of wilderness rivers, join the Sierra Club, write to the government, but turn off the lights you're not using, don't install an air conditioner, don't be a sucker for electrical gadgets, don't waste water. In other words, if you are fearful of the destruction of the environment, then learn to quit being an environmental parasite. We all are, in one way or another, and the remedies are not always obvious, though they certainly will always be difficult. They require a new kind of life—harder, more laborious, poorer in luxuries and gadgets, but also, I am certain, richer in meaning and more abundant in real pleasure. To have a healthy environment we will all have to give up things we like; we may even have to give up things we have come to think of as necessities. But to be fearful of the disease and yet unwilling to pay for the cure is not just to be hypocritical; it is to be doomed. If you talk a good line without being changed by what you say, then you are not just hypocritical and doomed; you have become an agent of the disease. Consider, for an example, President Nixon, who advertises his grave concern about the destruction of the environment, and who turns up the air conditioner to make it cool enough to build a fire.

Odd as I am sure it will appear to some, I can think of no better form of personal involvement in the cure of the environment than that of gardening. A person who is growing a garden, if he is growing it organically, is improving a piece of the world. He is producing something to eat, which makes him somewhat independent of the grocery business, but he is also enlarging, for himself, the meaning of food and the pleasure of eating. The food he grows will be fresher, more nutritious, less contaminated by poisons and preservatives and dyes than what he can buy at a store. He is reducing the trash problem; a garden is not a disposable container, and it will digest and re-use its own wastes. If he enjoys working in his garden, then he is less dependent on an automobile or a merchant for his pleasure. He is involving himself directly in the work of feeding people.

If you think I'm wandering off the subject, let me remind you that most of the vegetables necessary for a family of four can be grown on a plot of forty by sixty feet. I think we might see in this an economic potential of considerable importance, since we now appear to be facing the possibility of widespread famine. How much food could be grown in the dooryards of cities and suburbs? How much could be grown along the extravagant right-of-ways of the interstate system? Or how much could be grown, by the intensive practices and economics of the small farm, on so-called marginal lands? Louis Bromfield liked to point out that the people of France survived crisis after crisis because they were a nation of gardeners, who in times of want turned with great skill to their own small plots of ground. And F. H. King, an agriculture professor who traveled extensively in the Orient in 1907, talked to a Chinese farmer who supported a family of twelve, "one donkey, one cow . . . and two pigs on 2.5 acres of cultivated land"—and who did this, moreover, by agricultural methods that were sound enough organically to have maintained his land in prime fertility through several thousand years of such use. These are possibilities that are readily apparent and attractive to minds that are prepared to Think Little. To Big Thinkers—the bureaucrats and businessmen of agriculture—they are quite simply invisible. But intensive, organic agriculture kept the farms of the Orient thriving for thousands of years, whereas extensive—which is to say, exploitive or extractive—agriculture has critically reduced the fertility of American farmlands in a few centuries or even a few decades.

A person who undertakes to grow a garden at home, by practices that will preserve rather than exploit the economy of the soil, has set his mind decisively against what is wrong with us. He is helping himself in a way that dignifies him and that is rich in meaning and pleasure. But he is doing something else that is more important: he is making vital contact with the soil and the weather on which his life depends. He will no longer look upon rain as an impediment of traffic, or upon the sun as a holiday decoration. And his sense of man's dependence on the world will have grown precise enough, one would hope, to be politically clarifying and useful.

What I am saying is that if we apply our minds directly and competently to the needs of the earth, then we will have begun to make fundamental and necessary changes in our minds. We will begin to understand and to mistrust *and to change* our wasteful economy, which markets not just the produce of the earth, but also the earth's ability to produce. We will see that beauty and utility are alike dependent upon the health of the world. But we will also see through the fads and the fashions of protest. We will see that war and oppression and pollution are not separate issues, but are aspects of the same issue. Amid the outcries for the liberation of this group or that, we will know that no person is free except in the freedom of other persons, and that man's only real freedom is to know and faithfully occupy his place—a much humbler place than we have been taught to think—in the order of creation.

But the change of mind I am talking about involves not just a change of knowledge, but also a change of attitude toward our essential ignorance, a change in our bearing in the face of mystery. The principle of ecology, if we will take it to heart, should keep us aware that our lives depend upon other lives and upon processes and energies in an interlocking system that, though we can destroy it, we can neither fully understand nor fully control. And our great dangerousness is that, locked in our selfish and myopic economics, we have been willing to change or destroy far beyond our power to understand. We are not humble enough or reverent enough.

Some time ago, I heard a representative of a paper company refer to conservation as a "no-return investment." This man's thinking was exclusively oriented to the annual profit of his industry. Circumscribed by the demand that the profit be great, he simply could not be answerable to any other demand—not even to the obvious needs of his own children.

Consider, in contrast, the profound ecological intelligence of Black Elk, "a holy man of the Oglala Sioux," who in telling his story said that it was not his own life that was important to him, but what he had shared with all life: "It is the story of all life that is holy and it is good to tell, and of us two-leggeds sharing in it with the four-leggeds and the wings of the air and all green things. . . ." And of the great vision that came to him when he was a child he said: "I saw that the sacred hoop of my people was one of many hoops that made one circle, wide as daylight and as starlight, and in the center grew one mighty flowering tree to shelter all the children of one mother and father. And I saw that it was holy."

Discipline and Hope

I

Introductory Note

I begin with what I believe is a safe premise, at least in the sense that most of the various sides of the current public argument would agree, though for different reasons: that we have been for some time in a state of general cultural disorder, and that this disorder has now become critical. My interest here has been to examine to what extent this disorder is a failure of discipline—specifically, a failure of those disciplines, both private and public, by which desired ends might be reached, or by which the proper means to a desired end might be determined, or by which it might be perceived that one apparently desirable end may contradict or forestall another more desirable. Thus we have not asked how the "quality of life," as we phrase it, may be fostered by social and technological means that are sensitive only to quantitative measures; we have not really questioned the universal premise of power politics that peace (among the living) is the natural result of war; we have hardly begun to deal with the fact that an economy of waste is not compatible with a healthy environment.

I realize that I have been rather severely critical of several, perhaps all, sides of the present disagreement, having in effect made this a refusal to be a partisan of *any* side. There are some, I know, who will look upon such a refusal as a "cop-out." Obviously, I disagree. If critical intelligence has a use it is to prevent the coagulation of opinion in social or political cliques. My purpose has been to invoke the use of principle, rather than partisanship, as a standard of behavior, and to clear the rhetoric of the various sides from what ought to be the ground of personal experience and common sense.

It appears to me that the governing middle, or the government, which supposedly represents the middle, has allowed the extremes of left and right to force it into an extremism of its own. These three extremes of left, right, and middle, egged on by and helplessly subservient to each other's rhetoric, have now become so self-righteous and self-defensive as to have no social use. So large a ground of sanity and good sense and decency has been abandoned by these extremes that it becomes possible now to think of a New Middle made up of people conscious and knowledgeable enough to despise the blandishments and oversimplifications of the extremes—and roomy and diverse enough to permit a renewal of intelligent cultural dialogue. That is what I hope for: a chance to live and speak as a person, not as a function of some political bunch.

II

The Politics of Kingdom Come

Times of great social stress and change, when realities become difficult to face and to cope with, give occasion to forms of absolutism, demanding perfection. We are in such a time now, and it is producing the characteristic symptoms. It has suddenly become clear to us that practices and ambitions that we have been taught from the cradle to respect have made us the heirs apparent of a variety of dooms; some of the promised solutions, on which we have been taught to depend, are not working, are probably not going to work. As a result the country is burdened with political or cultural perfectionists of several sorts, demanding that the government or the people create *right now* one or another version of the ideal state. The air is full of dire prophecies, warnings, and threats of what will happen if the Kingdom of Heaven is not precipitately landed at the nearest airport.

It is important that we recognize the childishness of this. Its ancestor is the kicking fit of childhood, a sort of behavioral false rhetoric that offers the world two absolute alternatives: "If I can't have it, I'll tear it up." Its cultural model is the fundamentalist preacher, for whom there are no degrees of behavior, who cannot tell the difference between a shot glass and a barrel. The public *demand* for perfection, as opposed to private striving for it, is almost always productive of violence, and is itself a form of violence. It is totalitarian in impulse, and often in result.

The extremes of public conviction are always based upon rhetorical extremes, which is to say that their words —and their actions—have departed from facts, causes, and arguments, and have begun to follow the false logic of a feud in which nobody remembers the cause but only what was last said or done by the other side. Language and behavior become purely negative in function. The opponents no longer speak in support of their vision or their arguments or their purposes, but only in opposition to each other. Language ceases to bind head to heart, action to principle, and becomes a weapon in a contention deadly as war, shallow as a game.

But it would be an oversimplification to suggest that the present contention of political extremes involves only the left and the right. These contend not so much against each other as against the middle—the administration in power—which each accuses of *being* the other. In defending itself, the middle characteristically adopts the tactics of the extremes, corrupting its language by a self-congratulatory rhetoric bearing no more kinship to the truth and to honest argument than expediency demands, and thus it becomes an extreme middle. Whereas the extreme left and right see in each other the imminence of Universal Wrong, the extreme middle appears to sense in itself the imminence of the Best of All Possible Worlds, and therefore looks upon all critics as traitors. The rhetoric of the extreme middle equates the government with the country, loyalty to the government with patriotism, the will of the Chief Executive with the will of the people. It props itself with the tone of divine good will and infallibility, demanding an automatic unquestioning faith in its actions, upholding its falsehoods and errors with the same unblinking piety with which it obscures its truths and its accomplishments.

Because the extreme middle is characteristically in power, its characteristic medium is the one that is most popular—television. How earnestly and how well this middle has molded itself to the demands of television is apparent when one considers how much of its attention is given to image making, or remaking, and to public relations. It has given up almost altogether the disciplines of political discourse (considerations of fact and of principle and of human and historical limits and possibilities), and has taken up the cynical showmanship of those who have cheap goods for sale. Its catch phrases do not rise from any viable political tradition; their next of kin are the TV jingles of soup and soap. It is a politics of illusion, and its characteristic medium is pre-eminently suited—as it is almost exclusively limited—to the propagation of illusion.

Of all the illusions of television, that of its much-touted "educational value" is probably the first. Because of its utter transience as a medium and the complete passivity of its audience, television is doomed to have its effect within the limits of the most narrow and shallow definition of entertainment—that is, entertainment as diversion. The watcher sees the program at the expense of no effort at all; he is inert. All the live connections are broken. More important, a TV program can be seen only once; it cannot be re-examined or judged upon the basis of study, as even a movie can be. The report of a momentous event or a serious drama slips away from us among the ordinary furniture of our lives, as transient and fading as the most commonplace happenings of every day. For these reasons a political speech on television has to be first and last a show, simply because it has no chance to become anything else. The great sin of the medium is not that it presents fiction as truth, as undoubtedly it sometimes does, but that it cannot help presenting the truth as fiction, and that of the most negligible sort—a way to keep awake until bedtime.

In depending so much upon a medium that will not permit scrutiny, the extreme middle has perhaps naturally come to speak a language that will not *bear* scrutiny. It has thus abased its own part in the so-called political dialogue to about the level of the slogans and chants and the oversimplified invective of the extreme left and right—a fact that in itself might sufficiently explain the obsession with image making. Hearing the televised pronouncements of the political leaders of our time upon the great questions of human liberty, community obligation, war and peace, poverty and wealth, one might easily forget that once such highly disciplined and principled men as John Adams and Thomas Jefferson spoke here upon those questions. Indeed, our contemporary men of power have produced in their wake an industry of journalistic commentary and interpretation, because it is so difficult to determine *what* they have said and whether or not they meant it. Thus one sees the essential contradiction in the expedient doctrine that the end may justify the means. Corrupt or false means must inevitably corrupt or falsify the end. There is an important sense in which the end *is* the means.

What is disturbing, then, about these three "sides" of our present political life is not their differences but their similarities. They have all abandoned discourse as a means of clarifying and explaining and defending and implementing their ideas. They have taken almost exclusively to the use of the rhetoric of ad-writers: catch phrases, slogans, clichés, euphemisms, flatteries, falsehoods, and various forms of cheap wit. This has led them —as such rhetoric must—to the use of power and the use of violence against each other. But however their ideological differences might be graphed, they are, in effect, all on the same side. They are on the side of their quarrel, and are against all other, including all better, possibilities. There is a political and social despair in this that is the greatest peril a country can come to, short of the inevitable results of such despair should it continue very long. "We are fatalists," Edward Dahlberg wrote, "only when we cease telling the truth, but, so long as we communicate the truth, we move ourselves, life, history, men. There is no other way."

Our present political rhetoric is the desperation of argument. It is like a weapon in its inflexibility, in its insensitivity to circumstance, and in its natural inclination toward violence. It is by this recourse to loose talk—this willingness to say whatever will be easiest to say and most willingly heard—that the left permits its methods to contradict its avowed aims, as when it contemplates violence as a means of peace or permits arguments to shrink into slogans. By this process the right turns from its supposed aim of conserving the best of the past and undertakes the defense of economic privilege and the deification of symbols. And by this process the middle abandons its obligation to lead and enlighten the majority it claims as its constituency, and takes to the devices of a sterile showmanship, by which it hopes to elude criticism and obscure its failures.

The political condition in this country now is one in which the means or the disciplines necessary to the achievement of professed ends have been devalued or corrupted or abandoned altogether. We are offered peace without forbearance or tolerance or love, security without effort and without standards, freedom without risk or adventure, comfort without responsibility, abundance without thrift. We are asked repeatedly by our elected officials to console ourselves with that most degenerate of political arguments: though we are not doing as well as we might, we could do worse, and we are doing better than some.

III

The Kingdom of Efficiency and Specialization

But this political indiscipline is exemplary of a condition that is widespread and deeply rooted in almost all aspects of our life. Nearly all the old standards, which implied and required rigorous disciplines, have now been replaced by a new standard of efficiency, which requires not discipline, not a mastery of means, but rather a carelessness of means, a relentless subjection of means to immediate ends. The standard of efficiency displaces and destroys the standards of quality because, by definition, it cannot even consider them. Instead of asking a man what he can do well, it asks him what he can do fast and cheap. Instead of asking the farmer to practice the best husbandry, to be a good steward and trustee of his land and his art, it puts irresistible pressures on him to produce more and more food and fiber more and more cheaply, thereby destroying the health of the land, the best traditions of husbandry, and the farm population itself. And so when we examine the principle of efficiency as we now practice it, we see that it is not really efficient at all. As we use the word, efficiency means no such thing, or it means short-term or temporary efficiency; which is a contradiction in terms. It means cheapness at any price. It means hurrying to nowhere. It means the profligate waste of humanity and of nature. It means the greatest profit to the greatest liar. What we have called efficiency has produced among us, and to our incalculable cost, such unprecedented monuments of destructiveness and waste as the strip-mining industry, the Pentagon, the federal bureaucracy, and the family car.

Real efficiency is something entirely different. It is neither cheap (in terms of skill and labor) nor fast. Real efficiency is long-term efficiency. It is to be found in means that are in keeping with and preserving of their ends, in methods of production that preserve the sources of production, in workmanship that is durable and of high quality. In this age of consumerism, planned obsolescence, frivolous horsepower and surplus manpower, those salesmen and politicians who talk about efficiency are talking, in reality, about spiritual and biological death.

Specialization, a result of our nearly exclusive concern with the form of exploitation that we call efficiency, has in its turn become a destructive force. Carried to the extent to which we have carried it, it is both socially and ecologically destructive. That specialization has vastly increased our knowledge, as its defenders claim, cannot be disputed. But I think that one might reasonably dispute the underlying assumption that knowledge per se, undisciplined knowledge, is good. For while specialization has increased knowledge, it has fragmented it. And this fragmentation of knowledge has been accompanied by a fragmentation of discipline. That is, specialization has tended to draw the specialist toward the discipline that will lead to the discovery of new facts or processes within a narrowly defined area, and it has tended to lead him away from or distract him from those disciplines by which he might consider the *effects* of his discovery upon human society or upon the world. It has tended to value the disciplines that pertain to the gathering of knowledge and to its immediate use, and to devalue those that pertain to its ultimate effects.

Nowhere are these tendencies more apparent than in agriculture. For years now the agricultural specialists have tended to think and work in terms of piecemeal solutions and in terms of annual production, rather than in terms of a whole and coherent system that would maintain the fertility and the ecological health of the land over a period of centuries. Focused nearly exclusively upon so-called efficiency with respect to production, as if the only discipline pertinent to agriculture were that of economics, they have eagerly abetted a rapid industrialization of agriculture that is potentially catastrophic, both in the ecological deterioration of farm areas and in the dispossession and displacement of the rural population.

Ignoring the ample evidence that a healthy, ecologically sound agriculture is highly diversified, using the greatest possible variety of animals and plants, and that it returns all organic wastes to the soil, the specialists of the laboratories have promoted the specialization of the farms, encouraging one-crop agriculture and the replacement of humus by chemicals. And as the pressures of urban populations upon the land have grown, the specialists have turned more and more, not to the land, but to the laboratory.

Ignoring the considerable historical evidence that to have a productive agriculture over a long period of time it is necessary to have a stable and prosperous rural population closely bound in sympathy and association to the land, the specialists have either connived in the dispossession of small farmers by machinery and technology, or have actively encouraged their migration into the cities.

The result of the short-term vision of these experts is a whole series of difficulties that together amount to a rapidly building ecological and social disaster, which there is little disposition at present to regret, much less to correct. The organic wastes of our society, for which our land is starved and which in a sound agricultural economy would be returned to the land, are flushed out through the sewers to pollute the streams and rivers and, finally, the oceans; or they are burned and the smoke pollutes the air; or they are wasted in other ways. Similarly, the small farmers who in a healthy society ought to be the mainstay of the country—whose allegiance to their land, continuing and deepening in association from one generation to another, would be the motive and guarantee of good care—are forced out by the homicidal economics of efficiency, to become emigrants and dependents in the already overcrowded cities. In both instances, by the abuse of knowledge in the name of efficiency, assets have been converted into staggering problems.

The metaphor governing these horrendous distortions has been that of the laboratory. The working assumption has been that nature and society, like laboratory experiments, can be manipulated by processes that are for the most part comprehensible toward ends that are for the most part foreseeable. But the analogy, as any farmer would know instantly, is too simple, for both nature and humanity are vast in possibility, unpredictable and ultimately mysterious. Sir Albert Howard was speaking to this problem in *An Agricultural Testament*: "Instead of breaking up the subject into fragments and studying agriculture in piecemeal fashion by the analytical methods of science, appropriate only to the discovery of new facts, we must adopt a synthetic approach and look at the wheel of life as one great subject and not as if it were a patchwork of unrelated things." A much more appropriate model for the agriculturist, scientist, or farmer is the forest, for the forest, as Howard pointed out, "manures itself" and is therefore self-renewing; it has achieved that "correct relation between the processes of growth and the processes of decay that is the first principle of successful agriculture." A healthy agriculture can take place only within nature, and in co-operation with its processes, not in spite of it and not by "conquering" it. Nature, Howard points out, in elaboration of his metaphor, "never attempts to farm without live stock; she always raises mixed crops; great pains are taken to preserve the soil and to prevent erosion; the mixed vegetable and animal wastes are converted into humus; *there is no waste* [my emphasis]; the processes of growth and the processes of decay balance one another; ample provision is made to maintain large reserves of fertility; the greatest care is taken to store the rainfall; both plants and animals are left to protect themselves against disease."

The fact is that farming is not a laboratory science, but a science of practice. It would be, I think, a good deal more accurate to call it an art, for it grows not only out of factual knowledge but out of cultural tradition; it is learned not only by precept but by example, by apprenticeship; and it requires not merely a competent knowledge of its facts and processes, but also a complex set of attitudes, a certain culturally evolved stance, in the face of the unexpected and the unknown. That is to say, it requires *style* in the highest and richest sense of that term.

One of the most often repeated tenets of contemporary optimism asserts that "a nation that can put men on the moon certainly should be able to solve the problem of hunger." This proposition seems to me to have three important flaws, which I think may be taken as typical of our official view of ourselves:

1—It construes the flight to the moon as an historical event of a complete and coherent significance, when in fact it is a fragmentary event of very uncertain significance. Americans have gone to the moon as they came to the frontiers of the New World: with their minds very much upon getting there, very little upon what might be involved in *staying* there. I mean that because of our history of waste and destruction here, we have no assurance that we can survive in America, much less on the moon. And until we can bring into balance the processes of growth and decay, the white man's settlement of this continent will remain an incomplete event. When a Japanese peasant went to the fields of his tiny farm in the preindustrial age, he worked in the governance of an agricultural tradition that had sustained the land in prime fertility for thousands of years, in spite of the pressures of a population that in 1907 had reached a density, according to F. H. King's *Farmers of Forty Centuries,* of "more than three people to each acre." Such a farmer might look upon his crop year as a complete and coherent historical event, suffused and illuminated with a meaning and mystery that were both its own and the world's, because in his mind and work agricultural process had come into an enduring and preserving harmony with natural process. To him the past confidently promised a future. What are we to say, by contrast, of a society that places no value at all upon such a tradition or such a man, that instead works the destruction of such imperfect agricultural traditions as it has, that replaces the farm people with machines, that values the techniques of production far above the techniques of land maintenance, and that has espoused as an ideal a depopulated countryside farmed by a few technicians for the supposedly greater benefit of hundreds of millions crowded into cities and helpless to produce food or any other essential for themselves?

2—The agricultural optimism that bases itself upon the moon-landings assumes that there is an equation between agriculture and technology, or that agriculture is a kind of technology. This grows out of the much-popularized false assumptions of the agricultural specialists, who have gone about their work as if agriculture was answerable only to the demands of economics, not to those of ecology or human culture, just as most urban consumers conceive eating to be an activity associated with economics but not with agriculture. The ground of agricultural thinking is so narrowly circumscribed, one imagines, to fit the demands of laboratory science, as well as the popular prejudice that prefers false certainties to honest doubts. The discipline proper to eating, of course, is not economics but agriculture. The discipline proper to agriculture, which survives not just by production but also by the return of wastes to the ground, is not economics but ecology. And ecology may well find its proper disciplines in the arts, whose function is to refine and enliven *perception*, for ecological principle, however publicly approved, can be enacted only upon the basis of each man's perception of his relation to the world.

Under the governance of the laboratory analogy, the

device, which is simple and apparently simplifying, becomes the focal point and the standard rather than the human need, which is complex. Thus an agricultural specialist, prescribing the best conditions for the use of a harvesting machine, thinks only of the machine, not its cultural or ecological effects. And because of the fixation on optimum conditions, big-farm technology has come to be highly developed, whereas the technology of the family farm, which must still involve methods and economies that are "old-fashioned," has been neglected. For this reason, and others perhaps more pressing, small-farm technology is rapidly passing from sight, along with the small farmers. As a result we have an increasing acreage of supposedly "marginal" but potentially productive land for the use of which we have neither methods nor people—an alarming condition in view of the likelihood that someday we will desperately need to farm these lands again.

The drastic and incalculably dangerous assumption is that farming can be considered apart from farmers, that the land may be conceptually divided in its use from human need and human care. The assumption is that moving a farmer into a factory is as simple a cultural act as moving a worker from one factory to another. It is inconceivably more complicated, and more final. American agricultural tradition has been for the most part inadequate from the beginning, and we have an abundance of diminished land to show for it. But American farmers are nevertheless an agricultural population of long standing. Most settlers who farmed in America farmed in Europe. The farm population in this country therefore embodies a knowledge and a set of attitudes and interests that have been literally thousands of years in the making. This mentality is, or was, a great resource upon which we might have built a truly indigenous agriculture, fully adequate to the needs and demands of American regions. Ancient as it is, it is destroyed in a generation in every family that is forced off the farm into the city—or in less than a generation, for the farm mentality can survive only in sustained vital contact with the land.

A truer agricultural vision would look upon farming not as a function of the economy or even of the society, but as a function of the land; and it would look upon the farm population as an indispensable and inalienable part of the ecological system. Among the Incas, according to John Collier (*Indians of the Americas*), the basic social and economic unit was the tribe, or *ayllu*, but "the *ayllu* was not merely its people, and not merely the land, but people and land wedded through a mystical bond." The union of the land and the people was indissoluble, like marriage or grace. Chief Rekayi of the Tangwena tribe of Rhodesia, in refusing to leave his ancestral home, which had been claimed by the whites, is reported in recent newspaper accounts to have said: "I am married to this land. I was put here by God . . . and if I am to leave, I must be removed by God who put me here." This altogether natural and noble sentiment was said by the Internal Affairs Minister to have been "Communist inspired."

3—The notion that the moon voyages provide us assurance of enough to eat exposes the shallowness of our intellectual confidence, for it is based upon our growing inability to distinguish between training and education. The fact is that a man can be made an astronaut much more quickly than he can be made a good farmer, for the astronaut is produced by training and the farmer by education. Training is a process of conditioning, an orderly and highly efficient procedure by which a man learns a prescribed pattern of facts and functions. Education, on the other hand, is an obscure process by which a person's experience is brought into contact with his place and his history. A college can train a person in four years; it can barely begin his education in that time. A person's education begins before his birth in the making of the disciplines, traditions, and attitudes of mind that he will inherit, and it continues until his death under the slow, expensive, uneasy tutelage of his experience. The process that produces astronauts may produce soldiers and factory workers and clerks; it will never produce good farmers or good artists or good citizens or good parents.

White American tradition, so far as I know, contains only one coherent social vision that takes such matters into consideration, and that is Thomas Jefferson's. Jefferson's public reputation seems to have dwindled to that of Founding Father and advocate of liberty, author of several documents and actions that have been enshrined and forgotten. But in his thinking, democracy was not an ideal that stood alone. He saw that it would have to be secured by vigorous disciplines or its public offices would become merely the hunting grounds of mediocrity and venality. And so those who associate his name only with his political utterances miss both the breadth and depth of his wisdom. As Jefferson saw it, two disciplines were indispensable to democracy: on the one hand, education, which was to produce a class of qualified leaders, an aristocracy of "virtue and talents" drawn from all economic classes; and on the other hand, land, the widespread possession of which would assure stable communities, a tangible connection to the country, and a permanent interest in its welfare. In language that recalls Collier's description of the *ayllu* of the Incas, and the language of Chief Rekayi of the Tangwenans, Jefferson wrote that farmers "are tied to their country, and wedded to its liberty and interests, by the most lasting bonds." And: ". . . legislators cannot invent too many devices for subdividing property. . . ." And: ". . . it is not too soon to provide by every possible means that as few as possible shall be without a little portion of land. The small landholders are the most precious part of a state. . . ." For the discipline of education of the broad and humane sort that Jefferson had in mind, to produce a "natural aristocracy . . . for the instruction, the trusts, and government of society," we have tended more and more to substitute the specialized training that will most readily secure the careerist in his career. For the ownership of "a little portion of land" we have, and we apparently wish, to substitute the barbarous abstraction of nationalism, which puts our minds within the control of whatever demagogue can soonest rouse us to self-righteousness.

On September 10, 1814, Jefferson wrote to Dr. Thomas Cooper of the "condition of society" as he saw it at that time: ". . . we have no paupers, the old and crippled among us, who possess nothing and have no families to take care of them, being too few to merit no-

tice as a separate section of society. . . . The great mass
of our population is of laborers; our rich . . . being few,
and of moderate wealth. Most of the laboring class possess property, cultivate their own lands . . . and from
the demand for their labor are enabled . . . to be fed
abundantly, clothed above mere decency, to labor mod-
erately. . . . The wealthy . . . know nothing of what
the Europeans call luxury." This has an obvious kinship
with the Confucian formula: ". . . that the producers
be many and that the mere consumers be few; that the
artisan mass be energetic and the consumers temper-
ate . . ."

In the loss of that vision, or of such a vision, and in the
abandonment of that possibility, we have created a society characterized by degrading urban poverty and an
equally degrading affluence—a society of undisciplined
abundance, which is to say a society of waste.

IV

The Kingdom of Consumption

The results have become too drastic to be concealed by
our politicians' assurances that we have built a "great society" or that we are doing better than India. Official pretense has begun to break down under the weight of the
obvious. In the last decade we have become unable to
condition our children's minds to approve or accept our
errors. Our history has created in the minds of our young
people a bitter division between official pretense and so-

cial fact, and we have aggravated this division by asking many of them to fight and die in support of official pretense. In this way we have produced a generation whose dissidence and alienation are without precedent in our national experience.

The first thing to be said about this rebelliousness is that it is understandable, and that it deserves considerate attention. Many of this generation have rejected values and practices that they believe to be destructive, and they should do so. Many of them have begun to search for better values and forms of life, and they should do so. But the second thing to be said is that this generation is as subject as any other to intelligent scrutiny and judgment, and as deserving of honest criticism. It has received much approbation and condemnation, very little criticism.

One of its problems is that it has been isolated in its youthfulness, cut off from the experience and the counsel of older people, as probably no other generation has ever been. It is true that the dissident young have had their champions among the older people, but it is also true, I think, that these older people have been remarkably uncritical of the young, and so have abdicated their major responsibility to them. Some appear to have *joined* the younger generation, buying their way in by conniving in the myth that idealistic youth can do no wrong—or that one may reasonably hope to live without difficulty or effort or tragedy, or that surfing is "a life." The uncritical approval of a band of senior youth freaks is every bit as isolating and every bit as destructive as the uncritical condemnation of those who have made hair length the foremost social issue of the time.

And so a number of the problems of the young people now are problems that have always characterized youthfulness, but which isolation has tended to aggravate in the present generation: impetuousness, a haste to undertake work that one is not yet prepared for; a tendency to underestimate difficulty and overestimate possibility, which is apt, through disillusionment, to lead to the overestimation of difficulty and the underestimation of possibility; oversimplification, as when rejection takes the place of revaluation; and, finally, naïve prejudice, as when people who rightly condemn the use of such terms as "nigger" or "greaser" readily use such terms as "pig" and "redneck."

Another of its problems, and a much larger one, is that the propaganda both of the "youth culture" and of those opposed to it has inculcated in many minds, both young and old, the illusion that this is a wholly new generation, a generation free of history. The proposition is dangerously silly. The present younger generation is, as much as any other, a product of the past; it would not be as it is if earlier generations had not been as they were. Like every other young generation, this one bears the precious human burden of new possibility and new hope, the opportunity to put its inheritance to better use. And like every other, it also bears the germ of historical error and failure and weakness—which it rarely forgives in its predecessors, and seldom recognizes in itself. In the minds of those who do not know it well, and who have not mas-

tered the disciplines of self-criticism, historical error is a
subtle virus indeed. It is of the greatest importance that
we recognize in the youth culture the persistence in new
forms of the mentality of waste, certain old forms of
which many of the young have rightly repudiated.

Though it has forsworn many of the fashions and os-
tentations of the "affluent society," the youth culture
still supports its own forms of consumerism, the vener-
able American doctrine which holds that if enough is
good too much is better. As an example, consider the
present role of such drugs as marijuana and the various
hallucinogens. To deal sensibly with this subject, it is
necessary to say at the outset that the very concept of
drug abuse implies the possibility of drug use that is *not*
abusive. And it is, in fact, possible to produce examples
of civilizations that have employed drugs in disciplines
and ceremonies that have made them culturally useful
and prevented their abuse.

Tobacco, for instance, is a drug that we have used so
massively and thoughtlessly that we have, in typical fashion, come to feel threatened by it. This is the pattern of
the consumer economy and it applies not just to drugs,
but to such commodities as the automobile and electrical
power. But American Indians attached to tobacco a significance that made it more valuable to them than it has
ever been to us, and at the same time kept them from
misusing it as we have. In the Winnebago Origin Myth
tobacco had a ceremonial and theological role that
roughly parallels the role of Christ in Christian ceremony
and theology. According to this myth, Paul Radin wrote
in his Introduction to *The Road of Life and Death,*

man "is not to save himself or receive the wherewithal of life through the accidental benefactions of culture-heroes. On the contrary, he is to be in dire straits and saved. Earthmaker is represented as withholding tobacco from the spirits in order to present it to man and as endowing these same spirits with an overpowering craving for it. In short, it is to be the mechanism for an exchange between man and the deities. He will give them tobacco; they will give him powers to meet life and overcome obstacles."

The use of alcohol has had, I believe, a similar history: a decline and expansion from ceremonial use to use as a commodity and extravagance, from cultural usefulness to cultural liability.

The hallucinogenic drugs have now also run this course of cultural diminishment, and at the hands not of the salesmen of the corporations and the advertising agencies, but of the self-proclaimed enemies of those salesmen. Most of these drugs have been used by various cultures in association with appropriate disciplines and ceremonies. Anyone who reads an account of the dignified and beautiful Peyote Meeting of the Native American Church will see that it resembles very much the high ritual and art of other cultures but very little indeed the usual account of the contemporary "dope scene."

A very detailed and well-understood account of the disciplined use of such drugs is in Carlos Castenada's remarkable book, *The Teachings of Don Juan: A Yaqui Way of Knowledge*. Don Juan, a medicine man and sorcerer, a Yaqui Indian from Sonora, Mexico, undertakes to teach Castenada the uses of jimson weed, peyote, and the psilocybe mushrooms. The book contains some remarkable accounts of the author's visions under the influence of these drugs, but equally remarkable is the rigor of the disciplines and rituals by which his mentor prepared him for their use. At one point early in their association the old Indian said to him: "A man goes to knowledge as he goes to war, wide awake, with fear, with respect, and with absolute assurance. Going to knowledge or going to war in any other manner is a mistake, and whoever makes it will live to regret his steps."

The cultural role of both hallucinogens and intoxicants, in societies that have effectively disciplined their use, has been strictly limited. They have been used either for the apprehension of religious or visionary truth or, a related function, to induce in conditions prescribed by ceremony and festivity a state of self-abandon in which one may go free for a limited time of the obscuring and distorting preoccupation with one's own being. Other cultures have used other means—music or dance or poetry, for examples—to produce these same ends, and although the substance of Don Juan's teaching may be somewhat alien to the mainstream of our tradition, the terms of its discipline are not.

By contrast, the youth culture tends to use drugs in a way very similar to the way its parent culture uses alcohol: at random, as a social symbol and crutch, and with the emphasis upon the fact and quantity of use rather than the quality and the content of the experience. It would be false to say that these drugs have come into contemporary use without any of their earlier cultural associations. Indeed, a good deal of importance has been assigned to the "religious" aspect of the drug experience. But too often, it seems to me, the tendency has been to make a commodity of religion, as if in emulation of some churches. Don Juan looked upon drugs as a way to knowledge, difficult and fearful as other wise men have conceived other ways to knowledge, and therefore to be rigorously prepared for and faithfully followed; the youth culture, on the other hand, has tended to look upon drugs as a sort of instant Holy Truth, of which one need not become worthy. When they are inadequately prepared for the use of drugs, that is to say, people "consume" and waste them.

The way out of the wastefulness of consumerism obviously cannot lie simply in a shift from one fashionable commodity to another commodity equally fashionable. The way out lies only in a change of mind by which we will learn not to think of ourselves as consumers in any sense. A consumer is one who uses things up, a concept that is alien to the creation, as are the concepts of waste and disposability. A more realistic and creative vision of ourselves would teach us that our ecological obligations are to use, not use up; to use by the standard of real need, not of fashion or whim; and then to relinquish what we have used in a way that returns it to the common ecological fund from which it came.

The key to such a change of mind is the realization that the first and final order of the creation is not such an order as men can impose on it, but an order in the creation itself by which its various parts and processes sustain each other, and which is only to some extent understandable. It is, moreover, an order in which things find their places and their values not according to their inert substances, but according to their energies, their powers, by which they co-operate or affect and influence each other. The order of the creation, that is to say, is closer to that of drama than to that of a market.

This relation of power and order is another of the major concerns of the Winnebago Creation Myth. "Having created order within himself and established it for the stage on which man is to play," Paul Radin says, "Earthmaker proceeds to create the first beings who are to people the Universe, the spirits and deities. To each one he assigns a fixed and specific amount of power, to some more, to some less. . . . This principle of gradation and subordination is part of the order that Earthmaker is represented as introducing into the Universe. . . . The instant it is changed there is danger and the threat of disruption." The principle is dramatized, according to Radin, in the legend of Morning Star: ". . . one of the eight great Winnebago deities, Morning Star, has been decapitated by his enemy, a waterspirit. The body of the hero still remains alive and is being taken care of by his sister. The waterspirit, by keeping the head of Morning Star, has added the latter's power to his own. So formidable is this combination of powers that none of the deities [is] a match for him now. In fact only Earthmaker is his equal. Here is a threat of the first magnitude to the order ordained by Earthmaker and it must be met lest destruction overtake the world."

The point is obvious: to take and keep, to consume, the power of another creature is an act profoundly disordering, contrary to the nature of the creation. And equally obvious is its applicability to our own society, which sees its chief function in such accumulations of power. A man grows rich by strip mining, adding the power of a mountain to himself in such a way that he cannot give it back. As a nation, we have so far grown rich by adding the power of the continent to ourselves in such a way that we cannot give it back. "Here is a threat of the first magnitude to the order ordained by Earthmaker and it must be met lest destruction overtake the world."

Though we generally concede that a man may have more of the world's goods than he deserves, I think that we have never felt that a man may have more light than he deserves. But an interesting implication of the Winnebago doctrine of power and order is that a man must not only become worthy of enlightenment, but has also an ethical obligation to make himself worthy of the world's goods. He can make himself worthy of them only by using them carefully, preserving them, relinquishing them in good order when he has had their use. That a man shall find his life by losing it is an ethical concept that applies to the body as well as the spirit.

An aspect of the consumer mentality that has cropped up with particular virulence in the youth culture is an obsessive fashionableness. The uniformity of dress, hair style, mannerism, and speech is plain enough. But more serious, because less conscious and more pretentious, is an intellectual fashionableness pinned up on such shibboleths as "the people" (the most procrustean of categories), "relevance" (the most reactionary and totalitarian of educational doctrines), and "life style."

This last phrase furnishes a particularly clear example of the way poor language can obscure both a problem and the possibility of a solution. Compounded as "alternate life style," the phrase becomes a part of the very problem it aspires to solve. There are, to begin with, two radically different, even opposed meanings of style: style as fashion, an imposed appearance, a gloss upon superficiality; and style as the signature of mastery, the efflorescence of long discipline. It is obvious that the style of mastery can never become the style of fashion, simply because every master of a discipline is different from every other; his mastery is suffused with the nature of his own character and his own materials. Cézanne's paintings could not have been produced by a fad, for the simple reason that they could not have been produced by any other person. As a popular phrase, "life style" necessarily has to do only with what is imitable in another person's life, its superficial appearances and trappings; it cannot touch its substances, disciplines, or devotions. More important is the likelihood that a person who has identified his interest in another person as an interest in his "life style" will be *aware* of nothing but appearances. The phrase "alternate life style" attempts to recognize our great need to change to a kind of life that is not wasteful and destructive, but stifles the attempt, in the same breath, by infecting it with that superficial concept of style. An essential recognition is thus obscured at birth by the old lie of advertising and public relations: that you can alter substance by altering appearance. "Alternate life style" suggests, much in the manner of the fashion magazines, that one can change one's life by changing one's clothes.

Another trait of consumerism that thrives in the youth culture is that antipathy to so-called "drudgery" that has made us, with the help of salesmen and advertisers, a nation of suckers. This is the pseudoaristocratic notion, early popularized in America, that one is too good for the fundamental and recurring tasks of domestic order and biological necessity; to dirty one's hands in the soil or to submerge them for very long in soapy water is degrading and brutalizing. With one's hands thus occupied, the theory goes, one is unlikely to reach those elusive havens of "self-discovery" and "self-fulfillment"; but if one can escape such drudgery, one then has a fair chance of showing the world that one is *really* better than all previous evidence would have indicated. In every drudge there is an artist or a tycoon yearning to breathe free, a heart pregnant with celestial fire.

The entire social vision, as I understand it, goes something like this: man is born into a fallen world, doomed to eat bread in the sweat of his face. But there is an economic redemption. He should go to college and get an education—that is, he should acquire the "right" certificates and meet the "right" people. An education of this sort should enable him to get a "good" job—that is, short hours of work that is either easy or prestigious for a lot of money. Thus he is saved from the damnation of drudgery, and is presumably well on the way to proving the accuracy of his early suspicion that he is *really* a superior person.

Or, in a different version of the same story, the farmer at his plow or the housewife at her stove dreams of the neat outlines and the carefree boundaries of a factory worker's eight-hour day and forty-hour week, and his fat, unworried paycheck. They will leave their present drudgery to take the bait, in this case, of leisure, time, and money to enjoy the "good things of life."

In reality, this despised drudgery is one of the constants of life, like water only changing its form in response to changes of atmosphere. Our aversion to the necessary work that we call drudgery and our strenuous efforts to avoid it have not diminished it at all, but only degraded its forms. The so-called drudgery has to be done. If one is "too good" to do it for oneself, then it must be done by a servant, or by a machine manufactured by servants. If it is not done at home, then it must be done in a factory, which degrades both the conditions of work and the quality of the product. If it is not done well by the hands of one person, then it must be done poorly by the hands of many. But somewhere the hands of someone must be soiled with the work. Our aversion to this was once satisfied by slavery, or by the abuse of a laboring class; now it is satisfied by the assembly line, or by similar redundancy in bureaus and offices. For decades now our people have streamed into the cities to escape the drudgery of farm and household. Where do they go to escape the drudgery of the city? Only home at night, I am afraid, to the spiritual drudgery of factory-made suppers and TV. On weekends many of them continue these forms of urban drudgery in the country.

The youth culture has accepted, for the most part

uncritically, the conviction that all recurring and necessary work is drudgery, even adding to it a uniquely gullible acquiescence in the promoters' myth that the purpose of technology is to free mankind for spiritual and cultural pursuits. But to the older idea of economic redemption from drudgery, the affluent young have added the even more simple-minded idea of redemption by spontaneity. Do what you feel like, they say—as if every day one could "feel like" doing what is necessary. Any farmer or mother knows the absurdity of this. Human nature is such that if we waited to do anything until we felt like it, we would do very little at the start, even of those things that give us pleasure, and would do less and less as time went on. One of the common experiences of people who regularly do hard work that they enjoy is to find that they begin to "feel like it" only after the task is begun. And one of the chief uses of discipline is to assure that the necessary work gets done even when the worker *doesn't* feel like it.

Because of the prevalence of the economics and the philosophy of laborsaving, it has become almost a heresy to speak of hard work, especially manual work, as an inescapable human necessity. To speak of such work as good and ennobling, a source of pleasure and joy, is almost to declare oneself a pervert. Such work, and any aptitude or taste for it, are supposedly mere relics of our rural and primitive past—a past from which it is the business of modern science and technology to save us.

Before one can hope to use any intelligence in this matter, it is necessary to resurrect a distinction that was probably not necessary before the modern era, and that has so far been made only by a few eccentrics and renegades. It is a distinction not made in business and government, and very little made in the universities. I am talking about the distinction between work that is necessary and therefore meaningful, and work that is unnecessary or devoid of meaning. There is no intelligent defense of what Thoreau called "the police of meaningless labor." The unnecessary work of producing notions or trinkets or machines intended to be soon worn out, or necessary work the meaning of which has been destroyed by depersonalized process, is as degrading as slavery. And the purpose of such slavery, according to the laborsaving philosophy, is to set men free from work. Freed from work, men will presumably take to more "worthy" pursuits such as "culture." Noting that there have always been some people who, when they had leisure, studied literature and painting and music, the prophets of the technological paradise have always assured us that once we have turned all our work over to machines we will become a nation of artists or, at worst, a nation of art critics. This notion seems to me highly questionable on grounds both of fact and of principle.

In fact, we already know by experience what the "leisure" of most factory and office workers usually is, and we may reasonably predict that what it is it is likely to continue to be. Their leisure is a frantic involvement with salesmen, illusions, and machines. It is an expensive imitation of their work—anxious, hurried, unsatisfying. As their work offers no satisfactions in terms of work but must always be holding before itself the will-o'-the-wisp of freedom from work, so their leisure has no leisurely goals but must always be seeking its satisfaction outside itself, in some activity or some thing typically to be provided by a salesman. A man doing wholesome and meaningful work that he is pleased to do well is three times more at rest than the average factory or office worker on vacation. A man who does meaningless work does not have his meaning at hand. He must go anxiously in search of it—and thus fail to find it. The farmer's Sunday afternoon of sitting at home in the shade of a tree has been replaced by the "long weekend" of a thousand miles. The difference is that the farmer was where he wanted to be, understood the value of being there, and therefore when he had no work to do could sit still. How much have we spent to obscure so simple and obvious a possibility? The point is that there is an indissoluble connection and dependence between work and leisure. Meaningless work must produce meaningless leisure. The freedom from work must produce not leisure, but an ever more frantic search for something to do.

The principle was stated by Thoreau in his *Journal*: "Hard and steady and engrossing labor with the hands, especially out of doors, is invaluable to the literary man and serves him directly. Here I have been for six days surveying in the woods, and yet when I get home at evening, somewhat weary at last . . . I find myself more susceptible than usual to the finest influences, as music and poetry." That is, certainly, the testimony of an exceptional man, a man of the rarest genius, and it will be asked if such work could produce such satisfaction in an ordinary man. My answer is that we do not have to look far or long for evidence that all the fundamental tasks of feeding and clothing and housing—farming, gardening, cooking, spinning, weaving, sewing, shoemaking, carpentry, cabinetwork, stonemasonry—were once done with consummate skill by ordinary people, and as that skill indisputably involved a high measure of pride, it can confidently be said to have produced a high measure of satisfaction.

We are being saved from work, then, for what? The answer can only be that we are being saved from work that is meaningful and ennobling and comely in order to be put to work that is unmeaning and degrading and ugly. In 1930, the Twelve Southerners of *I'll Take My Stand* issued as an Introduction to their book "A Statement of Principles" in which they declared for the agrarian way of life as opposed to the industrial. The book, I believe, was never popular. At the time, and during the three decades that followed, it might have been almost routinely dismissed by the dominant cultural factions as an act of sentimental allegiance to a lost cause. But now it has begun to be possible to say that the cause for which the Twelve Southerners spoke in their Introduction was not a lost but a threatened cause: the cause of human civilization. "The regular act of applied science," they said, "is to introduce into labor a labor-saving device or a machine. Whether this is a benefit depends on how far it is advisable to save the labor. The philosophy of applied science is generally quite sure that the saving of labor is a pure gain, and that the more of it the better. This is to assume that labor is an evil, that only the end of labor or the material product is good. On this assumption labor becomes mercenary and servile. . . . The act of labor as one of the happy functions of human life has been in effect abandoned. . . .

"Turning to consumption, as the grand end which justifies the evil of modern labor, we find that we have been deceived. We have more time in which to consume, and many more products to be consumed. But the tempo of our labors communicates itself to our satisfactions, and these also become brutal and hurried. The constitution of the natural man probably does not permit him to shorten his labor-time and enlarge his consuming-time indefinitely. He has to pay the penalty in satiety and aimlessness."

The outcry in the face of such obvious truths is always that if they were implemented they would ruin the economy. The peculiarity of our condition would appear to be that the implementation of *any* truth would ruin the economy. If the Golden Rule were generally observed among us, the economy would not last a week. We have made our false economy a false god, and it has made blasphemy of the truth. So I have met the economy in the road, and am expected to yield it right of way. But I will not get over. My reason is that I am a man, and have a better right to the ground than the economy. The economy is no god to me, for I have had too close a look at its wheels. I have seen it at work in the strip mines and coal camps of Kentucky, and I know that it has no moral limits. It has emptied the country of the independent and the proud, and has crowded the cities with the dependent and the abject. It has always sacrificed the small to the large, the personal to the impersonal, the good to the cheap. It has ridden to its questionable triumphs over

the bodies of small farmers and tradesmen and craftsmen. I see it, still, driving my neighbors off their farms
into the factories. I see it teaching my students to give
themselves a price before they can learn to give themselves a value. Its principle is to waste and destroy the
living substance of the world and the birthright of posterity for a monetary profit that is the most flimsy and
useless of human artifacts.

Though I can see no way to defend the economy, I
recognize the need to be concerned for the suffering that
would be produced by its failure. But I ask if it is necessary for it to fail in order to change; I am assuming that if
it does not change it must sooner or later fail, and that a
great deal that is more valuable will fail with it. As a
deity the economy is a sort of egotistical French mon-
arch, for it apparently can see no alternative to itself except chaos, and perhaps that is its chief weakness. For, of
course, chaos is not the only alternative to it. A better
alternative is a better economy. But we will not conceive
the possibility of a better economy, and therefore will
not begin to change, until we quit deifying the present
one.

A better economy, to my way of thinking, would be
one that would place its emphasis not upon the *quantity*
of notions and luxuries but upon the *quality* of necessities. Such an economy would, for example, produce an
automobile that would last at least as long, and be at
least as easy to maintain, as a horse. It would encourage
workmanship to be as durable as its materials; thus a
piece of furniture would have the durability not of glue
but of wood. It would substitute for the pleasure of fri-

volity a pleasure in the high quality of essential work, in the use of good tools, in a healthful and productive countryside. It would encourage a migration from the cities back to the farms, to assure a work force that would be sufficient not only to the production of the necessary quantities of food, but to the production of food of the best *quality* and to the maintenance of the land at the highest fertility—work that would require a great deal more personal attention and care and hand labor than the present technological agriculture that is focused so exclusively upon production. Such a change in the economy would not involve large-scale unemployment, but rather large-scale changes and shifts of employment. Prices would no doubt increase, at least for a while, but they would also begin to reflect real values.

"You are tilting at windmills," I will be told. "It is a hard world, hostile to the values that you stand for. You will never enlist enough people to bring about such a change." People who talk that way are eager to despair, knowing how easy despair is. They want to give up all proper disciplines and all effort, and stand like cattle in a slaughterhouse, waiting their turn. The change I am talking about appeals to me precisely because it need not wait upon "other people." Anybody who wants to can begin it in himself and in his household as soon as he is ready—by becoming answerable to at least some of his own needs, by acquiring skills and tools, by learning what his real needs are, by refusing the merely glamorous and frivolous. When a person learns to *act* on his best hopes he enfranchises and validates them as no government or public policy ever will. And by his action the possibility that other people will do the same is made a likelihood.

But I must concede that there is also a sense in which I *am* tilting at windmills. While we have been preoccupied by various ideological menaces, we have been invaded and nearly overrun by windmills. They are drawing the nourishment from our soil and lifeblood out of our veins. I say let us tilt against the windmills. Though we have not conquered them, if we do not keep going at them they will surely conquer us.

V

The Kingdom of Abstraction and Organization

I do not wish to discount the usefulness of either abstraction or organization, but rather to point out that we have given them such an extravagant emphasis and such prodigal subsidies that their *functioning* has come to overbear and obscure and even nullify their usefulness. Their ascendency no doubt comes naturally enough out of the need to deal with the massive populations of an urban society. But their disproportionate, their almost exclusive, importance among us can only be explained as a disease of the specialist mentality that has found a haven in the government bureaus and the universities.

The bureaucrat who has formulated a plan, the specialist who has discovered a new fact or process, and the student who has espoused a social vision or ideal, all are of a kind in the sense that they all tend to think that they are at the end of a complete disciplinary process when in fact they have little more than reached the beginning of one. And this is their weakness: that they conceive abstractions to be complete in themselves, and therefore have only the simplest and most mechanical notions of the larger processes within which the abstractions will have their effect—processes that are apt, ultimately, to be obscure or mysterious in their workings and are therefore alien to the specialist mentality in the first place.

Having produced or espoused an abstraction, they next seek to put it to use by means of another abstraction—that is, an organization. But there is a sense in which organization is not a means of implementation, but rather a way of clinging to the clear premises and the neat logic of abstraction. The specialist mentality, unable by the terms of its narrow discipline to relinquish the secure order of abstraction, is prevented by a sort of Zeno's law from ever reaching the real ground of proof in the human community or in the world; it never *meets* the need it purports to answer. Demanding that each step toward the world be an orderly one, the specialist is by that very token not moving in the direction of the world at all, but on a course parallel to it. He can reach the world, not by any orderly process, but only by a reverse leap of faith from the ideal realm of the laboratory or theoretical argument onto the obscure and clumsifying ground of experience, where other and larger disciplines are required.

The man who must actually put the specialist's abstraction to use and live with its effects is never a part of the specialist organization. The organization can only deliver the abstraction to him and, of necessity, largely turn him loose with it. The farmer is not a part of the college of agriculture and the extension service; he is, rather, their object. The impoverished family is not a part of the welfare structure, but its object. The abstraction handed to these object-people is either true only in theory or it has been tried only under ideal (laboratory) conditions. For the bureaucrat, social planning replaces social behavior; for the agricultural scientist, chemistry and economics replace culture and ecology; for the political specialist (student or politician), theory replaces life, or tries to. Thus we institutionalize an impasse between the theoretical or ideal and the real, between the abstract and the particular; the specialist maintains a sort of esthetic distance between himself and the ground of proof and responsibility; and we delude ourselves that precept can have life and useful force without example.

Abstractions move toward completion only in the particularity of enactment or of use. Their completion is only in that mysterious whole that Sir Albert Howard and others have called the wheel of life. A vision or a principle or a discovery or a plan is therefore only *half* a discipline, and, practically speaking, it is the least important half. Black Elk, the holy man of the Sioux, said in his autobiography, *Black Elk Speaks*: "I think I have told you, but if I have not, you must have understood, that a man who has a vision is not able to use the power of it until after he has performed the vision on earth for the people to see." And only a few years later another American, William Carlos Williams, said much the same: "No ideas but in things." The difference of which both men spoke is that between knowledge and the *use* of knowledge. Similarly, one may speak of the difference between the production of an idea or a thing and its use. The disciplines of production are always small and specialized. The disciplines of use and continuity are both different and large. A man who produces a fact or an idea has not completed his responsibility to it until he sees that it is well used in the world. A man may grow potatoes as a specialist of sorts, but he falsifies himself and his potatoes too if he eats them and fails to live as a man.

If the culture fails to provide highly articulate connections between the abstract and the particular, the organizational and the personal, knowledge and behavior, production and use, the ideal and the world—that is, if it fails to bring the small disciplines of each man's work within the purview of those larger disciplines implied by the conditions of our life in the world—then the result is a profound disorder in which men release into their community and dwelling place powerful forces the consequences of which are unknown. New knowledge, political ideas, technological innovations, all are injected into society merely on the ground that to the specialists who produce them they appear to be good in themselves. A "laborsaving" device that does the work it was intended to do is thought by its developers to be a success: in terms of their discipline and point of view it *works*, it is operational. That, in working, it considerably lowers the quality of a product and makes obsolete a considerable number of human beings is, to the specialists, merely an opportunity for other specialists.

If this attitude were restricted to the elite of government and university it would be bad enough; but it has also been popularized by their propaganda and example to the extent that the general public is willing to attribute to declarations, promises, mere words, the force of behavior. We have allowed and even encouraged a radical disconnection between our words and our deeds. Our speech has drifted out of the world into a realm of fantasy in which whatever we say is true. The President of the republic openly admits that there is no connection between what he says and what he does—this in spite of his evident wish to be re-elected on the strength of what he says. We find it not extraordinary that lovers of America are strip mining in Appalachia, that lovers of peace are bombing villages in Southeast Asia, that lovers of freedom are underwriting dictatorships. If we *say* we are lovers of America and peace and freedom, then this must be what lovers of America and peace and freedom *do*. Having no need to account for anything they have done, our politicians do not find it necessary to trouble us with either evidence or argument, or to confess their errors, or to subtract their losses from their gains; they speak like the gods of Olympus, assured that if they *say* they are our servants anything they do in their own interest is right. Our public discourse has been reduced to the manipulation of uprooted symbols: good words, bad words, the names of gods and devils, emblems, slogans, flags. For some the flag no longer stands for the country, it *is* the country; they plant their crops and bury their dead in it.

There is no better example of this deterioration of language than in the current use of the word "freedom." Across the whole range of current politics this word is now being mouthed as if its devotees cannot decide whether it should be kissed or eaten, and this adoration has nothing to do with its meaning. The government is protecting the freedom of people by killing them or hiding microphones in their houses. The government's opponents, left and right, wish to set people free by telling them exactly what to do. All this is for the sake of the political power the word has come to have. The up-to-date politician no longer pumps the hand of a prospective constituent; he offers to set him—or her—free. And yet it seems to me that the word has no political meaning at all; the government cannot serve freedom except negatively—"by the alacrity," in Thoreau's phrase, "with which it [gets] out of its way."

The going assumption seems to be that freedom can be granted only by an institution, that it is the gift of the government to its people. I think it is the other way around. Free men are not set free by their government. Free men have set their government free of themselves; they have made it unnecessary. Freedom is not accomplished by a declaration. A declaration of freedom is either a futile and empty gesture, or it is the statement of a finished fact. As I understand it, freedom is a personal matter; though we may be enslaved as a group, we can be free only as persons. We can set each other free only as persons. It is a matter of discipline. A person can free himself of a bondage that has been imposed on him only by accepting another bondage that he has chosen. A man who would not be the slave of other men must be the master of himself—that is the real meaning of self-government. If we all behaved as honorably and honestly and as industriously as we expect our representatives to behave, we would soon put the government out of work.

A person dependent on somebody else for everything from potatoes to opinions may declare that he is a free man, and his government may issue a certificate granting him his freedom, but he will not be free. He is that variety of specialist known as a consumer, which means that he is the abject dependent of producers. How can he be free who can do nothing for himself? What is the First Amendment to him whose mouth is stuck to the tit of the "affluent society"? Men are free precisely to the extent that they are equal to their own needs. The most able are the most free.

VI

Discipline and Hope, Means as Ends

The various problems that I have so far discussed can best be understood, I think, as failures of discipline caused by a profound confusion as to the functions and the relative values of means and ends. I do not suggest simply that we fall with the ease of familiarity into the moral expedient of justifying means by ends, but that we have also come to attribute to ends a moral importance that far outweighs that which we attribute to means. As though we have arrived in our minds at a new age of fantasy or magic, we expect ends not only to justify means, but to rectify them as well. Once we have reached the desired end, we think, we will turn back to purify and consecrate the means. Once the war that we are fighting for the sake of peace is won, then the generals will become saints, the burned children will proclaim in heaven that their suffering is well repaid, the poisoned forests and fields will turn green again. Once we have peace, we say, or abundance or justice or truth or comfort, everything will be all right. It is an old dream.

It is a vicious illusion. For the discipline of ends is no discipline at all. The end is preserved in the means; a desirable end may perish forever in the wrong means. Hope lives in the means, not the end. Art does not survive in its revelations, or agriculture in its products, or craftsmanship in its artifacts, or civilization in its monuments, or faith in its relics.

That good ends are destroyed by bad means is one of the dominant themes of human wisdom. The *I Ching* says: "If evil is branded it thinks of weapons, and if we do it the favor of fighting against it blow for blow, we lose in the end because thus we ourselves get entangled in hatred and passion. Therefore it is important to begin at home, to be on guard in our own persons against the faults we have branded. . . . For the same reasons we should not combat our own faults directly. . . . As long as we wrestle with them, they continue victorious. Finally, the best way to fight evil is to make energetic progress in the good." Confucius said of riches that "if not obtained in the right way, they do not last." In the Sermon on the Mount, Jesus said: "Ye have heard that it hath been said, An eye for an eye, and a tooth for a tooth: But I say unto you, That ye resist not evil. . . ." And for that text Ken Kesey supplies the modern exegesis: "As soon as you resist evil, as soon as it's gone, you fold, because it's what you're based on." In 1931, Judge Lusk of the Chattanooga criminal court handed down a decision in which he wrote: "The best way, in my judgment, to combat Communism, or any other movement inimical to our institutions, is to show, if we can, that the injustices which they charge against us are, in fact, non-existent." And a friend of mine, a graduate of the University of Emily's Run, was once faced with the argument that he could "make money" by marketing some inferior lambs; he refused, saying that his purpose was the production of *good* lambs, and he would sell no other kind. He meant that his disciplines had to be those of a farmer, and that he would be diminished as a farmer by adopting the disciplines of a money-changer. It is a tragedy of our society that it neither pays nor honors a man for this sort of integrity—though it depends on him for it.

It is by now a truism that the great emphasis of our present culture is upon things, things as things, things in quantity without respect to quality; and that our predominant techniques and attitudes have to do with production and acquisition. We persist in the belief—against our religious tradition, and in the face of much evidence to the contrary—that if we leave our children wealthy we will assure their happiness. A corollary of this is the notion, rising out of the work of the geneticists, that we can assure a brighter future for the world by *breeding* a more intelligent race of humans—even though the present problems of the world are the result, not of human stupidity, but of human intelligence without adequate cultural controls. Both ideas are typical of the materialist assumption that human destiny can be improved by being constantly tinkered at, as if it were a sort of balky engine. But we can do nothing for the human future that we will not do for the human present. For the amelioration of the future condition of our kind we must look, not to the wealth or the genius of the coming generations, but to the quality of the disciplines and attitudes that we are preparing now for their use.

We are being virtually buried by the evidence that those disciplines by which we manipulate *things* are inadequate disciplines. Our cities have become almost unlivable because they have been built to be factories and vending machines rather than communities. They are conceptions of the desires for wealth, excitement, and ease—all illegitimate motives from the standpoint of community, as is proved by the fact that without the community disciplines that make for a stable, neighborly population, the cities have become scenes of poverty, boredom, and dis-ease.

The rural community—that is, the land and the people —is being degraded in complementary fashion by the specialists' tendency to regard the land as a factory and the people as spare parts. Or, to put it another way, the rural community is being degraded by the fashionable premise that the exclusive function of the farmer is production and that his major discipline is economics. On the contrary, both the function and the discipline of the farmer have to do with provision: he must provide, he must look ahead. He must look ahead, however, not in the economic-mechanistic sense of anticipating a need and fulfilling it, but in the sense of using methods that preserve the source. In his work sound economics becomes identical with sound ecology. The farmer is not a factory worker, he is the trustee of the life of the topsoil, the keeper of the rural community. In precisely the same way, the dweller in a healthy city is not an office or a factory worker, but part and preserver of the urban community. It is in thinking of the whole citizenry as factory workers—as readily interchangeable parts of an entirely mechanistic and economic order—that we have reduced our people to the most abject and aimless of nomads, and displaced and fragmented our communities.

An index of the health of a rural community—and, of course, of the urban community, its blood kin—might be found in the relative acreages of field crops and tree crops. By tree crops I mean not just those orchard trees of comparatively early bearing and short life, but also the fruit and nut and timber trees that bear late and live long. It is characteristic of an unsettled and anxious farm population—a population that feels itself, because of economic threat or the degradation of cultural value, to be ephemeral—that it farms almost exclusively with field crops, within economic and biological cycles that are complete in one year. This has been the dominant pattern of American agriculture. Stable, settled populations, assured both of an economic sufficiency in return for their work and of the cultural value of their work, tend to have methods and attitudes of a much longer range. Though they have generally also farmed with field crops, established farm populations have always been planters of trees. In parts of Europe, according to J. Russell

Smith's important book, *Tree Crops*, steep hillsides were covered with orchards of chestnut trees, which were kept and maintained with great care by the farmers. Many of the trees were ancient, and when one began to show signs of dying, a seedling would be planted beside it to replace it. Here is an agricultural discipline that could develop only among farmers who felt secure—as individuals and also as families and communities—in their connection to their land. Such a discipline depends not just on the younger men in the prime of their workdays but also on the old men, the keepers of tradition. The model figure of this agriculture is an old man planting a young tree that will live longer than a man, and that he himself may not live to see in its first bearing. And he is planting, moreover, a tree whose worth lies beyond any conceivable market prediction. He is planting it because the good sense of doing so has been clear to men of his place and kind for generations. The practice has been continued because it is ecologically and agriculturally sound; the economic soundness of it must be assumed. While the planting of a field crop, then, may be looked upon as a "short-term investment," the planting of a chestnut tree is a covenant of faith.

An urban discipline that in good health is closely analogous to healthy agriculture is teaching. Like a good farmer, a good teacher is the trustee of a vital and delicate organism: the life of the mind in his community. The ultimate and defining standard of his discipline is his community's health and intelligence and coherence and endurance. This is a high calling, deserving of a life's work. We have allowed it to degenerate into careerism and specialization. In education as in agriculture we have discarded the large and enlarging disciplines of community and place, and taken up in their stead the narrow and shallow discipline of economics. Good teaching is an investment in the minds of the young, as obscure in result, as remote from immediate proof as planting a chestnut seedling. But we have come to prefer ends that are entirely foreseeable, even though that requires us to foreshorten our vision. Education is coming to be, not a long-term investment in young minds and in the life of the community, but a short-term investment in the economy. We want to be able to tell how many dollars an education is worth and how soon it will begin to pay.

To accommodate these frivolous desires, education becomes training and specialization, which is to say, it institutionalizes and justifies ignorance and intellectual irresponsibility. It produces a race of learned mincers, whose propriety and pride it is to keep their minds inside their "fields," as if human thoughts were a kind of livestock to be kept out of the woods and off the roads. Because of the obsession with short-term results that may be contained within the terms and demands of a single life, the interest of community is displaced by the interest of career. The careerist teacher judges himself, and is judged by his colleagues, not by the influence he is having upon his students or the community, but by the size of his salary and the status of the place to which his career has taken him thus far. And, typically, he is where he is only temporarily; he is on his way to a more lucrative and prestigious place. Because so few stay around to be aware of the *effects* of their work, teachers are

not judged by their teaching, but by the short-term inci-
dentals of publication and "service." That teaching is a
long-term service, that a teacher's best work may be published in the children or grandchildren of his students,
cannot be considered, for the modern educator, like his
"practical" brethren in business and industry, will honor
nothing that he cannot see. That is not to say that books
do not have their progeny in the community, or that a
legitimate product of a teacher's life may not be a book.
It *is* to say that if *good* books are to be written, they will
be written out of the same resources of talent and discipline and character and delight as always, and not by institutional coercion.

It is not from the standpoint of the university itself
that we will see its faults, but from the standpoint of the
whole community. Looking only at the university, one
might perhaps believe that its first obligation is to become a better exemplar of its species: a *bigger* university,
with more prestigious professors publishing more books
and articles. But look at the state of Kentucky—whose
land is being vandalized and whose people are being impoverished by the absentee owners of coal; whose dispos-
sessed are hopeless refugees in the industrial cities to the
north; whose farm population and economy are under
the heaviest threat of their history; whose environment is
generally deteriorating; whose public schools have become legendary for their poor quality; whose public
offices are routinely filled by the morally incompetent.
Look at the *state* of Kentucky, and it is clear that, more
than any publication of books and articles, or any re-
search, we need an annual increment of several hundred

competently literate *graduates* who have some critical awareness of their inheritance and a sense of their obligation to it, and who know the use of books.

That, and that only, is the disciplining ideal of education, and the methods must be derived accordingly. It has nothing to do with number or size. It would be impossible to value economically; it is the antithesis of that false economy which thrives upon the exploitation of stupidity. It stands forever opposed to the assumption that you can produce a good citizen by subjecting a moral simpleton to specialized training or expert advice.

It is the obsession with immediate ends that is degrading, that destroys our disciplines, and that drives us to our inflexible concentration upon number and price and size. I believe that the closer we come to correct discipline, the less concerned we are with ends, and with questions of futurity in general. Correct discipline brings us into alignment with natural process, which has no explicit or deliberate concern for the future. We do not eat, for instance, because we want to live until tomorrow, but because we are hungry today and it *satisfies* us to eat. Similarly, a good farmer plants, not because of the abstractions of demand or market or his financial condition, but because it is planting time and the ground is ready— that is, he plants in response to his discipline and to his place. And the real teacher does not teach with reference to the prospective job market or some program or plan for the society's future; he teaches because he has something to teach and because he has students. A poet could not write a poem in order to earn a place in literary history. His place in literary history is another subject, and as such a distraction. He writes because he has a poem to write, he knows how, the work pleases him, and he has forgotten all else. "Take therefore no thought for the morrow: for the morrow shall take thought for the things of itself." This passage rests, of course, on the fact that we do not know what tomorrow will be, and are therefore strictly limited in our ability to take effective thought for it. But it also rests upon the assumption of correct disciplines. The man who works and behaves well today *need* take no thought for the morrow; he has discharged today's only obligation to the morrow.

VII

The Road and the Wheel

There are, I believe, two fundamentally opposed views of the nature of human life and experience in the world: one holds that though natural processes may be cyclic, there is within nature a human domain the processes of which are linear; the other, much older, holds that human life is subject to the same cyclic patterns as all other life. If the two are contradictory that is not so much because one is wrong and the other right as because one is partial and the other complete. The linear idea, of course, is the doctrine of progress, which represents man as having moved across the oceans and the continents and into space on a course that is ultimately logical and that will finally bring him to a man-made paradise. It also sees him as moving through time in this way, discarding old experience as he encounters new. The cyclic vision, on the other hand, sees our life ultimately not as a cross-country journey or a voyage of discovery, but as a circular dance in which certain basic *and necessary* patterns are repeated endlessly. This is the religious and ethical basis of the narrative of Black Elk: "Everything the Power of the World does is done in a circle. The sky is round, and I have heard that the earth is round like a ball, and so are all the stars. The wind, in its greatest power, whirls. Birds make their nests in circles, for theirs is the same religion as ours. The sun comes forth and goes down again in a circle. The moon does the same, and both are round. Even the seasons form a great circle in their changing, and always come back again to where they were. The life of a man is a circle from childhood to childhood, and so it is in everything where power moves. Our tepees were round like the nests of birds, and these were always set in a circle, the nation's hoop, a nest of many nests, where the Great Spirit meant for us to hatch our children." The doctrine of progress suggests that the fluctuations of human fortune are a series of ups and downs in a road tending generally upward toward the earthly paradise. To Black Elk earthly blessedness did not lie ahead or behind; it was the result of harmony within the circle of the people and between the people and the world. A man was happy or sad, he thought, in proportion as he moved toward or away from "the sacred hoop of [his] people [which] was one of many hoops that made one circle, wide as daylight and as starlight. . . ."

Characteristic of the linear vision is the idea that anything is justifiable only insofar as it is immediately and obviously good for something else. The linear vision tends to look upon everything as a cause, and to require that it proceed directly and immediately and obviously to its effect. What is it good for? we ask. And only if it proves immediately to be good *for* something are we ready to raise the question of value: How much is it worth? But we mean how much money, for if it can only be good for something else then obviously it can only be *worth* something else. Education becomes training as soon as we demand, in this spirit, that it serve some immediate purpose and that it be worth a predetermined amount. Once we accept so specific a notion of utility, all life becomes subservient to its use; its value is drained into its use. That is one reason why these are such hard times for students and old people: they are living either before or after the time of their greatest social utility. It is also the reason why so many non-human species are threatened with extinction. Any organism that is not contributing obviously and directly to the workings of the economy is now endangered—which means, as the ecologists are showing, that human society is to the same extent endangered. The cyclic vision is more accepting of mystery and more humble. Black Elk *assumes* that all things have a use—that is the condition of his respect for all things—but he does not know what all their uses are. Because he does not value them for their uses, he is free to value them for their own sake: "The Six Grandfathers have placed in this world many things, all of which should be happy. Every little thing is sent for something, and in that thing there should be happiness and the power to make happy." It should be emphasized that this is ecologically sound. The ecologists recognize that the creation is a great union of interlocking lives and processes and substances, all of which are dependent on each other; because they cannot discover the whole pattern of interdependency, they recognize the need for the greatest possible care in the use of the world. Black Elk and his people, however, were further advanced, for they possessed the cultural means for the enactment of a ceremonious respect for and delight in the lives with which they shared the world, and that respect and delight afforded those other lives an effective protection.

The linear vision looks fixedly straight ahead. It never looks back, for its premise is that there is no return. The doctrine of possession is complemented by no doctrine of relinquishment. Our shallow concept of use does not imply good use or preservation; thus quantity depresses quality, and we arrive at the concepts of waste and disposability. Similarly, life is lived without regard or respect for death. Death thus becomes accidental, the chance interruption of a process that might otherwise go on forever—therefore, always a surprise and always feared. Dr. Leon R. Kass, of the National Academy of Sciences, recently said that "medicine seems to be sharpening its tools to do battle with death as though death were just one more disease." The cyclic vision, at once more realistic and more generous, recognizes in the creation the essential principle of return: what is here will leave to come again; if there is to be having there must also be giving up. And it sees death as an integral and indispensable part of life. In one of the medicine rites of the Winnebago, according to Paul Radin, an old woman is made to voice this principle: "Our father has ordained that my body shall fall to pieces. I am the earth. Our father ordained that there should be death, lest otherwise there be too many people and not enough food for them." Because death is inescapable, a biological and ecological necessity, its acceptance becomes a spiritual obligation, the only means of making life whole: "Whosoever shall seek to save his life shall lose it; and whosoever shall lose his life shall preserve it."

The opposing characteristics of the linear and cyclic visions might, then, be graphed something like this:

Linear	*Cyclic*
Progress. The conquest of nature.	Atonement with the creation.
The Promised Land motif in the Westward Movement.	Black Elk's sacred hoop, the community of creation.
Heavenly aspiration without earthly reconciliation or stewardship. The creation as commodity.	Reconciliation of heaven and earth in aspiration toward responsible life. The creation as source *and end*.
Training. Programming.	Education. Cultural process.
Possession.	Usufruct, relinquishment.
Quantity.	Quality.
Newness. The unique and "original."	Renewal. The recurring.
Life.	Life and death.

The linear vision flourishes in ignorance or contempt of the processes on which it depends. In the face of these processes our concepts and mechanisms are so unrealistic, so *impractical*, as to have the nature of fantasy. The processes are invariably cyclic, rising and falling, taking and giving back, living and dying. But the linear vision places its emphasis entirely on the rising phase of the cycle—on production, possession, life. It provides for no returns. Waste, for instance, is a concept that could have been derived only from the linear vision. According to the scheme of our present thinking, every human activity produces waste. This implies a profound contempt for correct discipline; it proposes, in the giddy faith of prodigals, that there can be production without fertility, abundance without thrift. We take and do not give back, and this causes waste. It is a hideous concept, and it is making the world hideous. It is consumption, a wasting disease. And this disease of our material economy becomes also the disease of our spiritual economy, and we have made a shoddy merchandise of our souls. We want the truth to be easy and spectacular, and so we waste our verities; we are always hastening from the essential to the novel; we will have no prophet who is not an acrobat. We want to have love without a return of devotion or loyalty; to us, Aphrodite is a peeping statistician, the seismographer of orgasms. We want a faith that demands no return of good work. And art—we want it to be instantaneous and effortless; we want it to involve no apprenticeship to a tradition or a discipline or a master, no devotion to an ideal of workmanship. We want our art to support the illusion that high achievement is within easy reach, for we want to believe that, though we are demeaned by our work and driven half crazy by our pleasures, we are all mute inglorious Miltons.

To take up again my theme of agriculture, it is obvious that the modern practice concentrates almost exclusively on the productive phase of the natural cycle. The means of production become more elaborate all the time, but the means of return—the building of health and fertility in the soil—are reduced more and more to the shorthand of chemicals. According to the industrial vision of it, the life of the farm does not rise and fall in the turning cycle of the year; it goes on in a straight line from one harvest to another. This, in the long run, may well be more productive of waste than of anything else. It wastes the soil. It wastes the animal manures and other organic residues that industrialized agriculture frequently fails to return to the soil. And what may be our largest agricultural waste is not usually recognized as such, but is thought to be both an urban product and an urban problem: the tons of garbage and sewage that are burned or buried or flushed into the rivers. This, like all waste, is the abuse of a resource. It was ecological stupidity of exactly this kind that destroyed Rome. The chemist Justus von Liebig wrote that "the sewers of the immense metropolis engulfed in the course of centuries the prosperity of Roman peasants. The Roman Campagna would no longer yield the means of feeding her population; these same sewers devoured the wealth of Sicily, Sardinia and the fertile lands of the coast of Africa."

To recognize the magnitude and the destructiveness of our "urban waste" is to recognize the shallowness of the notion that agriculture is only another form of technology to be turned over to a few specialists. The sewage and garbage problem of our cities suggests, rather, that a healthy agriculture is a cultural organism, not merely a universal necessity but a universal obligation as well. It suggests that, just as the cities exist within the environment, they also exist within agriculture. It suggests that, like farmers, city-dwellers have agricultural responsibilities: to use no more than necessary, to waste nothing, to return organic residues to the soil.

Our ecological or agricultural responsibilities, then, call for a corresponding set of disciplines that would be a part of the cultural common ground, and that each person would have an obligation to preserve in his behavior. Seeking his own ends by the correct means, he transcends selfishness and makes a just return to the ecological source; by his correct behavior, both the source and the means for its proper use are preserved. This is equally true of other cultural areas: it is the discipline, not the desire, that is the common ground. In politics, for example, it is only the personal career that can be advanced by "image making." *Politics* cannot be advanced except by honest, informed, open discourse—by determining and telling and implementing the truth, by assuming the truth's heavy responsibilities and great risks. The political careerist, by serving his "image" rather than the truth, becomes a consumer of the political disciplines. Similarly, in art, the common ground is workmanship, the artistic means, the technical possibility of art—not the insights or visions of particular artists. A person who practices an art without mastering its disciplines becomes his art's consumer; he obscures the means, and encumbers his successors. The art lives *for* its insights and visions, but it cannot live *upon* them. An art is inherited and handed down in its workmanly aspects. Workmanship is the means by which the artist prepares for—becomes worthy of, earns—his vision and his insights. "Art," A. R. Ammons says, "is the conscious preparation for the unconscious event. . . ."

Learning the correct and complete disciplines—the disciplines that take account of death as well as life, decay as well as growth, return as well as production—is an indispensable form of cultural generosity. It is the one effective way a person has of acknowledging and acting upon the fact of mortality: he will die, others will live after him.

One reason, then, for the disciplinary weakness of the linear vision is that it is incomplete. Another is that it sees history as always leading not to renewal but to the new: the road may climb hills and descend into valleys, but it is always going ahead; it never turns back on itself. "We have constructed a fate . . . that never turns aside," Thoreau said of the railroad; "its orbit does not look like a returning curve. . . ." But when the new is assumed to be a constant, discipline fails, for discipline is preparation, and the new cannot be prepared for; it cannot, in any very meaningful way, be expected. Here again we come upon one of the reasons for the generational disconnections that afflict us: all times, we assume, are different; we therefore have nothing to learn from our elders, nothing to teach our children. Civilization is thus reduced to a sequence of last-minute improvisations, desperately building today out of the wreckage of yesterday.

There are two literary genres that seem to me to be characteristic (or symptomatic) of the linear vision. The first is, not prophecy, though it is sometimes called that, but the most mundane and inquisitive taking of thought for the morrow. What will tomorrow be like? (We mean, what new machines will be invented by then?) What will the world be like in ten or fifty or a hundred years? Our preoccupation with these questions, besides being useless, is morbid and scared; mistaking appearance for substance, it assumes a condition of *absolute* change: the future will be *entirely* different from the past and the present, we think, because our vision of history and experience has not taught us to imagine persistence or recurrence or renewal. We disregard the necessary persistence of ancient needs and obligations, patterns and cycles, and assume that the human condition is entirely determined by human *devices*.

The other genre—complementary, obviously—is that of the death sentence. Because we see the human situation as perpetually changing, the new bearing down with annihilating force, we appear to ourselves to be living always at the end of possibilities. For the new to happen, the old must be destroyed. Our own lives, which are pleasant to us at least insofar as they represent a *kind* of life that we recognize, seem always on the verge of being replaced by a kind of life that is unrecognizable, or by a death that is equally so. Thus a common theme for the writers of feature articles and critical essays is the death or the impending death of something: of the fashions of dress and appearance, of the novel, of printing, of freedom, of Christianity, of Western civilization, of the human race, of the world, of God.

This genre is difficult to criticize, because there is always a certain justice, or likelihood of justice, in it. There is no denying that we fear the end of things because our way of life has brought so many things to an end. The sunlit road of progress never escapes a subterranean dread that threatens to undermine the pavement. Thoreau knew that the railroad was built upon the bodies of Irishmen, and not one of us but secretly wonders when *he* will be called upon to lie down and become a sleeper beneath the roadbed of progress. And so some of this death-sentence literature is faithfully reporting the destructiveness of the linear vision; it is the chorus of accusation and dread and mourning that accompanies Creon's defiance of the gods.

But at times it is no more than one of the sillier manifestations of the linear vision itself: the failure to see any pattern in experience, the failure to transform experience into useful memory. There is a sort of journalistic greenness in us that is continuously surprised by the seasons and the weather, as if these were no more than the inventions (or mistakes) of the meteorologists. History, likewise, is always a surprise to us; we read its recurring disasters as if they were the result merely of miscalculations of our intelligence—as if they could not have been foreseen in the flaws of our character. And the heralds of the push-button Eden of the future would be much put off to consider that those button-pushers will still have to deal with problems of food and sewage, with the picking up of scraps and the disposal of garbage, with building and maintenance and reclamation—with, that is, the fundamental work, much of it handwork, that is necessary to civilization; they would be even more put off to consider that the quality of life will not depend nearly so much on the distribution of pushbuttons as on the manner and the quality of that fundamental and endlessly necessary work.

Some cycles revolve frequently enough to be well known in a man's lifetime. Some are complete only in the memory of several generations. And others are so vast that their motion can only be assumed: like our galaxy, they appear to us to be remote and exalted, a Milky Way, when in fact they are near at hand, and we and all the humble motions of our days are their belongings. We are kept in touch with these cycles, not by technology or politics or any other strictly human device, but by our necessary biological relation to the world. It is only in the processes of the natural world, and in analogous and related processes of human culture, that the new may grow usefully old, and the old be made new.

The ameliorations of technology are largely illusory. They are always accompanied by penalties that are equal and opposite. Like the weather reports, they suggest the possibility of better solutions than they can provide; and by this suggestiveness—this glib and shallow optimism of gimcrackery—they have too often replaced older skills that were more serviceable to life in a mysterious universe. The farmer whose weather eye has been usurped by the radio has become less observant, has lost his old judicious fatalism with respect to the elements—and he is no more certain of the weather. It is by now obvious that these so-called blessings have not made us better or wiser. And their expense is growing rapidly out of proportion to their use. How many plastic vitals can the human race afford? How many mountains can the world afford to the strip miners, to light the whole outdoors and overheat our rooms? The limits, as Thoreau knew, have been in sight from the first: "To make a railroad round the world available to all mankind," he said in *Walden*, "is equivalent to grading the whole surface of the planet. Men have an indistinct notion that if they keep up this activity of joint stocks and spades long enough all will at length ride . . . but though a crowd rushes to the depot . . . when the smoke is blown away and the vapor condensed, it will be perceived that a few are riding, but the rest are run over. . . ."

We cannot look for happiness to any technological paradise or to any New Earth of outer space, but only to the world as it is, and as we have made it. The only life we may hope to live is here. It seems likely that if we are to reach the earthly paradise at all, we will reach it only when we have ceased to strive and hurry so to get there. There is no "there." We can only wait here, where we are, in the world, obedient to its processes, patient in its taking away, faithful to its returns. And as much as we may know, and all that we deserve, of earthly paradise will come to us.

VIII

Kinds of Discipline

The disciplines we most readily think of are technical; they are the means by which we define and enact our relationship to the creation, and destroy or preserve the commonwealth of the living. There is no disputing the importance of these, and I have already said a good deal in their support. But alone, without the larger disciplines of community and faith, they fail of their meaning and their aim; they cannot even continue for very long. People who practice the disciplines of workmanship for their own sake—that is, as specializations—begin a process of degeneracy in those disciplines, for they remove from them the ultimate sense of use or effect by which their vitality and integrity are preserved. Without a proper sense of use a discipline declines from community responsibility to personal eccentricity; cut off from the common ground of experience and need, vision escapes into wishful or self-justifying fantasy, or into greed. Artists lose the awareness of an audience, craftsmen and merchants lose the awareness of customers and users.

Community disciplines, which can arise only out of the cyclic vision, are of two kinds. First there is the discipline of principle, the essence of the experience of the historical community. And second there is the discipline of fidelity to the living community, the community of family and neighbors and friends. As our society has become increasingly rootless and nomadic, it has become increasingly fashionable among the rhetoricians of dissatisfaction to advocate, or to seem to advocate, a strict and solitary adherence to principle in simple defiance of other people. "I don't care what they think" has become public currency with us; saying it, we always mean to imply that we are persons solemnly devoted to high principle—rugged individuals in the somewhat fictional sense Americans usully give to that term. In fact, this ready defiance of the opinions of others is a rhetorical fossil from our frontier experience. Once it meant that if our neighbors' opinions were repugnant to us, we were prepared either to kill our neighbors or to move west. Now it doesn't mean anything; it is adolescent bluster. For when there is no frontier to retreat to, the demands of one's community will be felt, and ways must be found to deal with them. The great moral labor of any age is probably not in the conflict of opposing principles, but in the tension between a living community and those principles that are the distillation of its experience. Thus the present anxiety and anguish in this country have very little to do with the much-heralded struggle between capitalism and communism, and very much indeed to do with the rapidly building discord and tension between American principles and American behavior.

This sort of discord is the subject of tragedy. It is tragic because—outside the possibility of a renewal of harmony, which may depend upon the catharsis of tragedy—there are no possible resolutions that are not damaging. To choose community over principle is to accept in consequence a diminishment of the community's moral inheritance; it is to accept the great dangers and damages of life without principle. To choose principle over community is even worse, it seems to me, for that is to accept as the condition of being "right" a solitude in which the right is ultimately meaningless; it is to destroy the only ground upon which principle can be enacted, and renewed; it is to raise an ephemeral hope upon the ground of final despair.

Facing exactly this choice between principle and community, on April 20, 1861, Robert E. Lee resigned his commission in the army of the United States. Lee had clearly understood the evil of slavery. He disapproved and dreaded secession; almost alone among the Virginians, he foresaw the horrors that would follow. And yet he chose to go with his people. Having sent in his resignation, he wrote his sister: ". . . though I recognize no necessity for this state of things, and would have forborne and pleaded to the end for a redress of grievances, real or supposed, yet in my own person I had to meet the question whether I should take part against my native state. With all my devotion to the Union and the feeling of loyalty and duty of an American citizen, I have not been able to make up my mind to raise my hand against my relatives, my children, my home."

He was right. As a highly principled man, he could not bring himself to renounce the very ground of his principles. And devoted to that ground as he was, he held in himself much of his region's hope of the renewal of principle. His seems to me to have been an exemplary American choice, one that placed the precise Jeffersonian vision of a rooted devotion to community and homeland above the abstract "feeling of loyalty and duty of an American citizen." It was a tragic choice on the theme of Williams' maxim: "No ideas but in things."

If the profession of warfare has so declined in respectability since 1861 as to obscure my point, then change the terms. Say that a leader of our own time, in spite of his patriotism and his dependence on "the economy," nevertheless held his people and his place among them in such devotion that he would not lie to them or sell them shoddy merchandise or corrupt their language or degrade their environment. Say, in other words, that he would refuse to turn his abilities against his people. That is what Lee did, and there have been few public acts of as much integrity since.

It is the intent of community disciplines, of course, to prevent such radical conflicts. If these disciplines are practiced at large among the members of the community, then the community holds together upon a basis of principle that is immediately clarified in feeling and behavior; and then destructive divisions, and the moral agony of exceptional men, are averted.

In the Sermon on the Mount a major concern is with the community disciplines. The objective of this concern is a social ideal: ". . . all things whatsoever that men should do to you, do ye even so to them. . . ." But that everyone would do as he would be done by is hardly a realistic hope, and Jesus was speaking out of a moral tradition that was eminently realistic and tough-minded. It was a tradition that, in spite of its heavenly aspirations, was very worldly in its expectations: it would have spared Sodom for the sake of ten righteous men. And so the focus of the Sermon is not on the utopian social ideal of the Golden Rule, but on the *personal* ideal of nonresistance to evil: ". . . whosoever shall smite thee on thy right cheek, turn to him the other also. . . . Love your enemies, bless them that curse you, do good to them that hate you, and pray for them which despitefully use you, and persecute you. . . ." The point, I think, is that the anger of one man need not destroy the community, if it is contained by the peaceableness and long-suffering of another, but in the anger of *two* men, in anger repaid—"An eye for an eye, and a tooth for a tooth"—it is destroyed altogether.

Community, as a discipline, extends and enlarges the technical disciplines by looking at them within the perspective of their uses or effects. Community discipline imposes upon our personal behavior an ecological question: What is the effect, on our neighbors and on our place in the world, of what we do? It is aware that *all* behavior is social. It is aware, as the ecologists are aware, that there is a unity in the creation, and that the behavior and the fate of one creature must therefore affect the whole, though the exact relationships may not be known.

But essential as are the disciplines of technique and community, they are not sufficient in themselves. All such disciplines reach their limit of comprehension, and at that point enter mystery. Thus an essential part of a discipline is that relinquishment or abandonment by which we acknowledge and accept its limits. We do not finally know what will be the result of our actions, however correct and excellent they may be. The good work we do today may be undone by some mere accident tomorrow. Our neighborly acts may be misunderstood and repaid with anger. With respect to what is to come, our real condition is that of abandonment; one of the primary functions of religion is to provide the ceremonial means of acknowledging this: we are in the hands of powers that we do not know.

The ultimate discipline, then, is faith: faith, if in nothing else, in the propriety of one's disciplines. We have obscured the question of faith by pretending that it is synonymous with the question of "belief," which is personal and not subject to scrutiny. But if one's faith is to have any public validity or force, then obviously it must meet some visible test. The test of faith is consistency—not the fanatic consistency by which one repudiates the influence of knowledge, but rather a consistency between principle and behavior. A man's behavior should be the creature of his principles, not the creature of his circumstances. The point has great practical bearing, because belief and the principles believed in, and whatever hope and promise are implied in them, are destroyed in contradictory behavior; hypocrisy salvages nothing but the hypocrite. If we put our faith in the truth, then we risk everything—the truth included—by telling lies. If we believe in the power of reason, then we risk everything by carrying a club. If we believe in peace, then we must see that violence makes us infidels. When we institute repressions to protect democracy from enemies abroad, we have already damaged it at home. The demands of faith are absolute: we must put all our eggs in one basket; we must burn our bridges.

An exemplary man of faith was Gideon, who reduced

his army from thirty-two thousand to three hundred in earnest of his trust, and marched that remnant against the host of the Midianites, armed, not with weapons, but with "a trumpet in every man's hand, with empty pitchers, and lamps within the pitchers."

Beside this figure of Gideon, the hero as man of faith, let us place our own "defender," the Pentagon, which has faith in nothing except its own power. That, as the story of Gideon makes clear, is a dangerous faith for mere men; it places them in the most dangerous moral circumstance, that of *hubris*, in which one boasts that "mine own hand hath saved me." To be sure, the Pentagon is supposedly founded upon the best intentions and the highest principles, and there is a plea that justifies it in the names of Christianity, peace, liberty, and democracy. But the Pentagon is an institution, not a person; and unless constrained by the moral vision of persons in them, institutional ambitions run in the direction of power and self-preservation, not high principle. Established, allegedly, in defense of "the free world," the Pentagon subsists complacently upon the involuntary servitude of millions of young men whose birthright, allegedly, is freedom. To wall our enemies out, it is walling us in.

Because its faith rests entirely in its own power, its mode of dealing with the rest of the world is not faith but suspicion. It recognizes no friends, for it knows that the face of friendship is the best disguise of an enemy. It has only enemies, or prospective enemies. It must therefore be prepared for *every possible* eventuality. It sees the future as a dark woods with a gunman behind every tree. It is passing through the valley of the shadow of death without a shepherd, and thus is never still. But as long as it can keep the public infected with its own state of mind, this spiritual dis-ease, it can survive without justification, and grow huge. Whereas the man of faith may go armed with only a trumpet and an empty pitcher and a lamp, the institution of suspicion arms with the death of the world; trusting nobody, it must stand ready to kill everybody.

The moral is that those who have no faith are apt to be much encumbered by their equipment, and overborne by their precautions. For the institution of suspicion there is no end of toiling and spinning. The Pentagon exists continually, not only on the brink of war, but on the brink of the exhaustion of its moral and material means. But the man of faith, even in the night, in the camp of his enemies, is at rest in the assurance of his trust and the correctness of his ways. He has become the lily of the field.

IX

The Likenesses of Atonement (At-one-ment)

Living in our speech, though no longer in our consciousness, is an ancient system of analogies that clarifies a series of mutually defining and sustaining unities: of farmer and field, of husband and wife, of the world and God. The language both of our literature and of our everyday speech is full of references and allusions to this expansive metaphor of farming and marriage and worship. A man planting a crop is like a man making love to his wife, and vice versa: he is a husband or a husband-man. A man praying is like a lover, or he is like a plant in a field waiting for rain. As husbandman, a man is both the steward and the likeness of God, the greater hus-bandman. God is the lover of the world and its faithful husband. Jesus is a bridegroom. And he is a planter; his words are seeds. God is a shepherd and we are his sheep. And so on.

All the essential relationships are comprehended in this metaphor. A farmer's relation to his land is the basic and central connection in the relation of humanity to the creation; the agricultural relation *stands for* the larger re-lation. Similarly, marriage is the basic and central com-munity tie; it begins and stands for the relation we have to family and to the larger circles of human association. And these relationships to the creation and to the human community are in turn basic to, and may stand for, our relationship to God—or to the sustaining mysteries and powers of the creation.

(These three relationships are dependent—and even intent—upon renewals of various sorts: of season, of fer-tility, of sexual energy, of love, of faith. And these con-cepts of renewal are always accompanied by concepts of loss or death; in order for the renewal to take place, the old must be not forgotten but relinquished; in order to become what we may be, we must cease to be as we are; in order to leave life we must lose it. Our language bears abundant testimony to these deaths: the year's death that precedes spring; the burial of the seed before germina-tion; sexual death, as in the Elizabethan metaphor; death as the definitive term of marriage; the spiritual death that must precede rebirth; the death of the body that must precede resurrection.)

As the metaphor comprehends all the essential relationships, so too it comprehends all the essential moralities. The moralities are ultimately emulative. For the metaphor does not merely perceive the likeness of these relationships. It perceives also that they are understandable only in terms of each other. They are the closed system of our experience; no instructions come from outside. A man finally cannot act upon the basis of absolute law, for the law is more fragmentary than his own experience; finally, he must emulate in one relationship what he knows of another. Thus, if the metaphor of atonement is alive in his consciousness, he will see that he should love and care for his land as for his wife, that his relation to his place in the world is as solemn and demanding, and as blessed, as marriage; and he will see that he should respect his marriage as he respects the mysteries and transcendent powers—that is, as a sacrament. Or—to move in the opposite direction through the changes of the metaphor—in order to care properly for his land he will see that he must emulate the Creator: to learn to use and preserve the open fields, as Sir Albert Howard said, he must look into the woods; he must study and follow natural process; he must understand the *husbanding* that, in nature, always accompanies providing.

Like any interlinking system, this one fails in the failure of any one of its parts. When we obscure or corrupt our understanding of any one of the basic unities, we begin to misunderstand all of them. The vital knowledge dies out of our consciousness and becomes fossilized in our speech and our culture. This is our condition now. We have severed the vital links of the atonement metaphor, and we did this initially, I think, by degrading and obscuring our connection to the land, by looking upon the land as merchandise and ourselves as its traveling salesmen.

I do not know how exact a case might be made, but it seems to me that there is an historical parallel, in white American history, between the treatment of the land and the treatment of women. The frontier, for instance, was notoriously exploitive of both, and I believe for largely the same reasons. Many of the early farmers seem to have worn out farms and wives with equal regardlessness, interested in both mainly for what they would produce, crops and dollars, labor and sons; they clambered upon their fields and upon their wives, struggling for an economic foothold, the having and holding that cannot come until both fields and wives are properly cherished. And today there seems to me a distinct connection between our nomadism (our "social mobility") and the nearly universal disintegration of our marriages and families.

The prevalent assumption appears to be that marriage problems are problems strictly of "human relations": if the husband and wife will only assent to a number of truisms about "respect for the other person," "giving and taking," et cetera, and if they will only "understand" each other, then it is believed that their problems will be solved. The difficulty is that marriage is only partly a matter of "human relations," and only partly a circumstance of the emotions. It is also, and as much as anything, a practical circumstance. It is very much under the influence of things and people outside itself; that is, it must make a household, it must make a place for itself in the world and in the community. But with us, getting someplace always involves going somewhere. Every professional advance leads to a new place, a new house, a new neighborhood. Our marriages are always being cut off from what they have made; their substance is always disappearing into the thin air of human relations.

I think there is a limit to the portability of human relationships. Tribal nomads, when they moved, moved as a tribe; their personal and cultural identity—their household and community—accompanied them as they went. But our modern urban nomads are always moving away from the particulars by which they know themselves, and moving into abstraction (*a* house, *a* neighborhood, *a* job) in which they can only feel threatened by new particulars. The marriage becomes a sort of assembly-line product, made partly here and partly there, the whole of it never quite coming into view. Provided they stay married (which is unlikely) until the children leave (which is usually soon), the nomadic husband and wife who look to see what their marriage has been—that is to say, what it *is*—are apt to see only the lines in each other's face.

The carelessness of place that must accompany our sort of nomadism makes a vagueness in marriage that is its antithesis. And vagueness in marriage, the most sacred human bond and perhaps the basic metaphor of our moral and religious tradition, cannot help but produce a diminishment of reverence, and of the care for the earth that must accompany reverence.

When the metaphor of atonement ceases to be a live function of our consciousness, we lose the means of relationship. We become isolated in ourselves, and our behavior becomes the erratic destructive behavior of people who have no bonds and no limits.

X

The Practicality of Morals

What I have been preparing at such length to say is that there is only one value: the life and health of the world. If there is only one value, it follows that conflicts of value are illusory, based upon perceptual error. Moral, practical, spiritual, esthetic, economic, and ecological values are all concerned ultimately with the same question of life and health. To the virtuous man, for example, practical and spiritual values are identical; it is only corruption that can see a difference. Esthetic value is always associated with sound values of other kinds. "Beauty is truth, truth beauty," Keats said, and I think we may take him at his word. Or to say the same thing in a different way: beauty is wholeness; it is health in the ecological sense of amplitude and balance. And ecology is long-term economics. If these identities are not apparent immediately, they are apparent *in time*. Time is the merciless, infallible critic of the specialized disciplines. In the ledgers that justify waste the ink is turning red.

Moral value, as should be obvious, is not separable from other values. An adequate morality would be ecologically sound; it would be esthetically pleasing. But the point I want to stress here is that it would be *practical*. Morality is long-term practicality.

Of all specialists the moralists are the worst, and the processes of disintegration and specialization that have characterized us for generations have made moralists of us all. We have obscured and weakened morality, first, by advocating it for its own sake—that is, by deifying it, as esthetes have deified art—and then, as our capacity for reverence has diminished, by allowing it to become merely decorative, a matter of etiquette.

What we have forgotten is the origin of morality in fact and circumstance; we have forgotten that the nature of morality is essentially practical. Moderation and restraint, for example, are necessary, not because of any religious commandment or any creed or code, but because they are among the assurances of good health and a sufficiency of goods. Likewise, discipline is necessary if the necessary work is to be done; also if we are to know transport, transcendence, joy. Loyalty, devotion, faith, self-denial are not ethereal virtues, but the concrete terms upon which the possibility of love is kept alive in this world. Morality is neither ethereal nor arbitrary; it is the definition of what is humanly possible, and it is the definition of the penalties for violating human possibility. A person who violates human limits is punished or he pre-

pares a punishment for his successors, not necessarily because of any divine or human law, but because he has
transgressed the order of things. A live and adequate morality is an accurate perception of the order of things, and
of humanity's place in it. By clarifying the human limits,
morality tells us what we risk when we forsake the human to behave like false gods or like animals.

One would not wish to say—indeed, it is precisely my
point that one *should* not say—that social *forms* will not
change with changing conditions. They probably *will* do
so, wholly regardless of whether or not they *should*. But I
believe that it is erroneous to assume that a change of
form implies a change of discipline. Under the influence
of the rapid changes of modern life, it is persistently assumed that we are moving toward a justifiable relaxation
of disciplines. This is wishful thinking, and it invites ca-
lamity, for the human place in the order of things, the
human limits, the human tragedy remain essentially the
same. It seems altogether possible, as a final example,
that for various reasons the forms of marriage will
change. But this does not promise a new age of benefit
without obligation—which, I am afraid, is what many
people mean by freedom. Though the forms of marriage
may change, if it continues to exist in any form it will
continue to rest upon the same sustaining disciplines,
and to incorporate the same tragic awareness: that it is
made "for better for worse, for richer for poorer, in sickness and in health, to love and to cherish, till
death. . . ."

XI

The Spring of Hope

The most destructive of ideas is that extraordinary times justify extraordinary measures. This is the ultimate relativism, and we are hearing it from all sides. The young, the poor, the colored races, the Constitution, the nation, traditional values, sexual morality, religious faith, Western civilization, the economy, the environment, the world are all now threatened with destruction—so the arguments run—therefore let us deal with our enemies by whatever means are handiest and most direct; in view of our high aims history will justify and forgive. Thus the violent have always rationalized their violence.

But as wiser men have always known, all times are extraordinary in precisely this sense. In the condition of mortality all things are always threatened with destruction. The invention of atomic holocaust and the other man-made dooms, though it changes the agent and the means, only restores for us the immediacy of the worldly circumstance as the religions have always defined it: we know "neither the day nor the hour. . . ."

Our bewilderment is not the time but our character. We have come to expect too much from outside ourselves. If we are in despair or unhappy or uncomfortable, our first impulse is to assume that this cannot be our fault; our second is to assume that some institution is not doing its duty. We are in the curious position of expecting from others what we can only supply ourselves. One of the Confucian ideals is that the "archer, when he misses the bullseye, turns and seeks the cause of the error in himself."

Goodness, wisdom, happiness, even physical comfort, are not institutional conditions. Institutions may perhaps promote them somewhat, but only negatively, by not interfering with them. The real sources of hope are personal and spiritual, not public and political. A man is not happy by the dispensation of his government or by the fortune of his age. He is happy only in doing well what is in his power, and in being reconciled to what is not in his power. Thoreau, who knew such happiness, wrote in "Life Without Principle": "Of what consequence, though our planet explode, if there is no character involved in the explosion? In health we have not the least curiosity about such events. We do not live for idle amusement. I would not run round a corner to see the world blow up."

Asked one day why the Shakers, who expected the end of the world at any moment, were nevertheless consummate farmers and craftsmen, Thomas Merton replied: "When you expect the world to end at any moment, you know there is no need to hurry. You take your time, you do your work well."

In Defense of Literacy

In a country in which everybody goes to school, it may seem absurd to offer a defense of literacy, and yet I believe that such a defense is in order, and that the absurdity lies not in the defense, but in the necessity for it. The published illiteracies of the certified educated are on the increase. And the universities seem bent upon ratifying this state of things by declaring the acceptability, in their graduates, of adequate—that is to say, of mediocre—writing skills.

The schools, then, are following the general subservience to the "practical," as that term has been defined for us according to the benefit of corporations. By "practicality" most users of the term now mean whatever will most predictably and most quickly make a profit. Teachers of English and literature have either submitted, or are expected to submit, along with teachers of the more "practical" disciplines, to the doctrine that the purpose of education is the mass production of producers and consumers. This has forced our profession into a predicament that we will finally have to recognize as a perversion. As if awed by the ascendency of the "practical" in our society, many of us secretly fear, and some of us are apparently ready to say, that if a student is not going to become a teacher of his language, he has no need to master it.

In other words, to keep pace with the specialization—and the dignity accorded to specialization—in other disciplines, we have begun to look upon and to teach our language and literature as specialties. But whereas specialization is of the nature of the applied sciences, it is a perversion of the disciplines of language and literature. When we understand and teach these as specialties, we submit willy-nilly to the assumption of the "practical men" of business, and also apparently of education, that literacy is no more than an ornament: when one has become an efficient integer of the economy, *then* it is permissible, even desirable, to be able to talk about the latest novels. After all, the disciples of "practicality" may someday find themselves stuck in conversation with an English teacher.

I may have oversimplified that line of thinking, but not much. There are two flaws in it. One is that, among the self-styled "practical men," the practical is synonymous with the immediate. The long-term effects of their values and their acts lie outside the boundaries of their interest. For such people a strip mine ceases to exist as soon as the coal has been extracted. Short-term practicality is long-term idiocy.

The other flaw is that language and literature are always *about* something else, and we have no way to predict or control what they may be about. They are about the world. We will understand the world, and preserve ourselves and our values in it, only insofar as we have a language that is alert and responsive to it, and careful of it. I mean that literally. When we give our plows such brand names as "Sod Blaster," we are imposing on their use conceptual limits which raise the likelihood that they will be used destructively. When we speak of man's "war against nature," or of a "peace offensive," we are accepting the limitations of a metaphor that suggests, and even proposes, violent solutions. When students ask for the right of "participatory input" at the meetings of a faculty organization, they are thinking of democratic process, but they are *speaking* of a convocation of robots, and are thus devaluing the very traditions that they invoke.

Ignorance of books and the lack of a critical consciousness of language were safe enough in primitive societies with coherent oral traditions. In our society, which exists in an atmosphere of prepared, public language—language that is either written or being read—illiteracy is both a personal and a public danger. Think how constantly "the average American" is surrounded by premeditated language, in newspapers and magazines, on signs and billboards, on TV and radio. He is forever being asked to buy or believe somebody else's line of goods. The line of goods is being sold, moreover, by men who are trained to make him buy it or believe it, whether or not he needs it or understands it or knows its value or wants it. This sort of selling is an honored profession

among us. Parents who grow hysterical at the thought
that their son might not cut his hair are *glad* to have him
taught, and later employed, to lie about the quality of an
automobile or the ability of a candidate.

What is our defense against this sort of language—this
language-as-weapon? There is only one. We must know a
better language. We must speak, and teach our children
to speak, a language precise and articulate and lively
enough to tell the truth about the world as we know it.
And to do this we must know something of the roots and
resources of our language; we must know its literature.
The only defense against the worst is a knowledge of
the best. By their ignorance people enfranchise their
exploiters.

But to appreciate fully the necessity for the best sort
of literacy we must consider not just the environment of
prepared language in which most of us now pass most of
our lives, but also the utter transience of most of this
language, which is meant to be merely glanced at, or
heard only once, or read once and thrown away. Such
language is by definition, and often by calculation, not
memorable; it is language meant to be replaced by what
will immediately follow it, like that of shallow conversation between strangers. It cannot be pondered or effectively criticized. For those reasons an unmixed diet of it is
destructive of the informed, resilient, critical intelligence
that the best of our traditions have sought to create and
to maintain—an intelligence that Jefferson held to be indispensable to the health and longevity of freedom. Such
intelligence does not grow by bloating upon the ephemeral information and misinformation of the public

media. It grows by returning again and again to the landmarks of its cultural birthright, the works that have proved worthy of devoted attention.

"Read not the Times. Read the Eternities," Thoreau said. Ezra Pound wrote that "literature is news that STAYS news." In his lovely poem, "The Island," Edwin Muir spoke of man's inescapable cultural boundaries and of his consequent responsibility for his own sources and renewals:

Men are made of what is made,
The meat, the drink, the life, the corn,
Laid up by them, in them reborn.
And self-begotten cycles close
About our way; indigenous art
And simple spells make unafraid
The haunted labyrinths of the heart . . .

These men spoke of a truth that no society can afford to shirk for long: we are dependent, for understanding, and for consolation and hope, upon what we learn of ourselves from songs and stories. This has always been so, and it will not change.

I am saying, then, that literacy—the mastery of language and the knowledge of books—is not an ornament, but a necessity. It is impractical only by the standards of quick profit and easy power. Longer perspective will show that it alone can preserve in us the possibility of an accurate judgment of ourselves, and the possibilities of correction and renewal. Without it, we are adrift in the present, in the wreckage of yesterday, in the nightmare of tomorrow.

Mayhem in the
Industrial Paradise

*. . . they have made my pleasant field a
desolate wilderness. . . .*

—JEREMIAH 12:10

I have just spent two days flying over the coal fields of
both eastern and western Kentucky, looking at the works
of the strip miners. Several times before, I had driven
and walked to look at strip mines, mainly in the eastern
part of the state, but those earlier, ground-level experiences did not prepare me at all for what I saw from the
air. In scale and desolation—and, I am afraid, in duration
—this industrial vandalism can be compared only with
the desert badlands of the West. The damage has no human scale. It is a geologic upheaval. In some eastern
Kentucky counties, for mile after mile after mile, the
land has been literally hacked to pieces. Whole mountain tops have been torn off and cast into the valleys.
And the ruin of human life and possibility is commensu-
rate with the ruin of the land. It is a scene from the Book
of Revelation. It is a domestic Vietnam.

174

So far as I know, there are only two philosophies of land use. One holds that the earth is the Lord's, or it holds that the earth belongs to those yet to be born as well as to those now living. The present owners, according to this view, only have the land in trust, both for all the living who are dependent on it now, and for the unborn who will be dependent on it in time to come. The model of this sort of use is a good farm—a farm that, by the return of wastes and by other safeguards, preserves the land in production without diminishing its ability to produce. The standard of this sort of land use is fertility, which preserves the interest of the future.

The other philosophy is that of exploitation, which holds that the interest of the present owner is the only interest to be considered. The standard, according to this view, is profit, and it is assumed that whatever is profitable is good. The most fanatical believers in the rule of profit are the strip miners. The earth, these people would have us believe, is not the Lord's, nor do the unborn have any share in it. It belongs, instead, to rich organizations with names like Peabody, Kentucky River Coal, Elkhorn Coal, National Steel, Bethlehem Steel, Occidental Petroleum, The Berwind Corporation, Tennessee Valley Authority, Chesapeake & Ohio, Ford Motor Company, and many others. And the earth, they would say, is theirs not just for a time, but forever, and in proof of their claim they do not hesitate to destroy it forever—that is, if it is profitable to do so, and earth-destruction has so far been exceedingly profitable to these organizations.

The gospel of the strip miners is the "broad form deed," under which vast acreages of coal rights were bought up for as little as twenty-five and fifty cents an acre before modern strip-mine technology ever had been conceived. The broad form deed holds that the coal may be taken out "in any and every manner that may be deemed necessary or convenient for mining. . . ." Kentucky is one of the few coal states that still honor the broad form deed. In Kentucky, under the sanction of this deed, the strip miners continue to ravage other people's private property. They have overturned or covered up thousands of acres of farm and forest land; they have destroyed the homes and the burial grounds of the people; they have polluted thousands of miles of streams with silt and mine acid; they have cast the overburden of the mines into the water courses and into the public roads. Their limits are technological, not moral. They have made it plain that they will stop at nothing to secure the profit, which is their only motive. And in Kentucky they have been aided and abetted at every turn by lawmakers, judges, and other public officials who are too cowardly or too greedy to act in the interest of those they are sworn to protect. Though the violations of the inadequate strip-mine regulations passed by the legislature have been numerous and well publicized, the regulations have been weakly enforced.

If the model of good land use is to be found in a good farm, then it is a strange sort of farming indeed that is practiced by these strip miners, whose herds are not cattle eating grass, but machines devouring the earth. That sounds fantastical, but then strip mining is an industry *based* upon fantasy. It proceeds upon the assumption that there is no law of gravity, that no heavy rains will fall, that water and mud and rock will not move downhill, that money is as fertile as topsoil, that the wealthy do not ultimately share the same dependences and the same fate as the poor, that the oppressed do not turn against their oppressors—that, in other words, there are no natural or moral or social consequences. Such are the luxuries that our society affords to the warlords of the exploitive industries.

People who live nearer to the results of strip mining know better. Those whose homes and belongings have been destroyed, or who live beneath the spoil banks, or who inhabit the flood plains of mutilated streams and rivers, or who have been driven into ruin and exile—and there are now many thousands of them—they know that the costs are inconceivably greater than any shown on coal-company ledgers, and they are keeping their own accounts. They know that the figment of legality that sanctions strip mining is contrary to the laws of nature and of morality and of history. And they know that in such a contradiction is the seed of social catastrophe.

The most vicious fantasy of all is the endlessly publicized notion that the net profit of the coal companies somehow represents the net profit of the whole society. Historically, however, the enrichment of the coal interests in Kentucky has always involved the impoverishment of the people of the mining regions. And of all methods of mining, strip mining is the most enriching to the rich and the most impoverishing to the poor; it has fewer employees and more victims. The net profit is net only to the coal companies, only on the basis of an annual accounting. The corporate profit is reckoned on so short a term. But the public expenditure that supports this private profit is long-term; the end of it is not now foreseeable. By the time all the reclaimable mined lands are reclaimed, and all the social and environmental damages accounted for, strip mining will be found to have been the most extravagantly subsidized adventure ever undertaken.

An estimate of the public meaning of strip-mine profits may be made from the following sentences by James Branscome in the New York *Times* of December 12, 1971: "The Corps of Engineers has estimated . . . that it would cost the public $26-million to restore the extensively strip-mined Coal River watershed in West Virginia. This is an amount approximately equal to the private profit taken by the mining companies from the watershed." But even this may be too limited an accounting. It does not consider the environmental damage, or the property damage, that may have occurred outside the boundaries of the immediate watershed between the opening of the coal seam and the completion of reclamation. It does not attempt to compute the cost of what may have been the permanent degradation of the appearance and the fertility of the land. Nor does it consider the economic consequences of the social upheaval that must always accompany an upheaval of the environment. There is, then, every reason to believe that the large net profit of a strip-mine company will prove to be a large net loss to society.

This, as all Kentuckians should be aware, is largely the responsibility of absentee owners. Of the thirty-three largest owners of mineral rights in the Kentucky coal fields, as recently listed by the *Courier-Journal*, only two are based in the state. But even those owners who live in the state are absentee owners in the strict sense of the term: they do not live with the consequences of what they do. As exploitive industrialists have done from the beginning, they live apart, in enclaves of the well-to-do, where they are neither offended nor immediately threatened by the ugliness and the dangers that they so willingly impose upon others. It is safe, I think, to say that not many coal-company executives and stockholders are living on the slopes beneath the spoil banks of their mines; not many of them have had their timber uprooted and their farms buried by avalanches of overburden; not many of them have had their water supply polluted by mine acid, or had their houses torn from the foundations by man-made landslides; not many of them see from their doorsteps the death of the land of their forefathers and the wreckage of their own birthright; not many of them see in the faces of their wives and children the want and the grief and the despair with which the local people subsidize the profits of strip mining. On the contrary, the worries of the coal companies are limited strictly to coal. When the coal is gone they do not care what is left. The inescapable conclusion is that Kentucky has been made a colony of the coal companies, who practice here a mercantilism as heartless and greedy as any in history.

In this new year* the state's lawmakers have once again assembled in Frankfort. Again they have the oppor-

---

* 1972.

tunity to put a stop to this awful destruction, and to assure to the state the benefits of its own wealth, and to give to the people of the coal fields the same protections of the law that are enjoyed by people everywhere else. If the men in power will do these things that are so clearly right and just, they will earn the gratitude of the living and of the unborn. If they will not do them, they will be infamous, and will be unworthy of the respect of any honest citizen.*

Remembering the new deserts of this once bountiful and beautiful land, my mind has gone back repeatedly to those Bible passages that are haunted by the memory of good land laid waste, and by fear of the human suffering that such destruction has always caused. Our own time has come to be haunted by the same thoughts, the same sense of a fertile homeland held in the contempt of greed, sold out, and destroyed. Jeremiah would find this evil of ours bitterly familiar:

I brought you into a fruitful land
    to enjoy its fruit and the goodness of it;
    but when you entered upon it you defiled it
    and made the home I gave you loathsome.

The damages of strip mining are justified in the name of electrical power. We need electrical power, the argument goes, to run our factories, to heat and light and air-condition our homes, to run our household appliances, our TV sets, our children's toys, and our mechanical

---

* They did not do them, and they are as unworthy of respect as I said they would be.

toothbrushes. And we must have more and more electricity because we are going to have more and more gadgets that will make us more and more comfortable. This, of course, is the reasoning of a man eating himself to death. We have to begin to distinguish between the uses that are necessary and those that are frivolous. Though it is the last remedy that would occur to a glutton or a coal company, we must cut down on our consumption—that is, our destruction—of the essential energies of our planet. We must use these energies less and with much greater care. We must see the difference between the necessity of warmth in winter and the luxury of air conditioning in the summer, between light to read or work by and those "security lights" with which we are attempting to light the whole outdoors, between an electric sewing machine and an electric toothbrush. Immediate comfort, we must say to the glutton, is no guarantee of a long life; too much now is, rather, a guarantee of too little later on. Our comfort will be paid for by someone else's distress. "We dig coal to light your tree," said a recent advertisement of the coal industry. That, we must realize, is not a Christmas greeting, but a warning of our implication in an immitigable evil.

In the name of Paradise, Kentucky, and in its desecrations by the strip miners, there is no shallow irony. It was named Paradise because, like all of Kentucky in the early days, it was recognized as a garden, fertile and abounding and lovely; some pioneer saw that it was good. ("Heaven," said one of the frontier preachers, "is a Kentucky of a place.") But the strip miners have harrowed Paradise, as they would harrow heaven itself were they to find coal there. Where the little town once stood in the shade of its trees by the riverbank, there is now a blackened desert. We have despised our greatest gift, the inheritance of a fruitful land. And for such despite—for the destruction of Paradise—there will be hell to pay.